Busi
Purpose
Design

Monika
Smith

An essential guide
for human-centric
and holistic businesses

For readability reasons there is no parallel use of male and female expressions. All terms used throughout to denote persons refer to both gender.

This work, including all individual parts, is protected by copyright. Every use without the approval of the publisher is illegal. This particularly applies to reproductions, translations, microfilming and storing and processing in electronic systems.

2nd edition

Copyright © 2020
Monika Smith

Publisher:
Santiago Berlin GmbH
www.sanitagoberlin.com

ISBN 978-3-9819249-4-7

hello@business-purpose.com
www.businesspurpose.design

Editors for German Version:
Antje Dohmann
Jennifer Giwi
Christoph Koch
Alexander Langer
Jakob von Lindern
Martin Mühl

Editors for English Version:
Peta Jenkin
Madeleine LaRue

Art Direction and Layout:
T. S. Wendelstein
The Simple Society
www.thesimplesociety.com

Layout:
Malwine Stauss

Illustration:
Johanna Benz, Tiziana Jill Beck
Graphic Recording Cool
www.graphicrecording.cool

Lead-Author	Monika Smith	**Purpose Facilitator, Leadership Coach and Consultant**
Authors	Dr. Maren Beverung	**Consultant and Facilitator**
	Scot Carlson	**Digital Transformation Lead at Reprise Digital**
	Pascal Fantou	**Growth Hacker and Founder Q48**
	Curt Simon Harlinghausen	**Serial Entrepreneur, Nerd, Growth Hacker, Digital Creative und 101010**
	Daniel Heltzel	**Managing Director Fab Lab Berlin**
	Steffan Heuer	**US-Correspondent of brand eins magazine**
	Philip Siefer	**Co-Founder of Einhorn Products**
	Martin Sinner	**Entrepreneur and Investor**
	Christian Solmecke	**Lawyer and Partner of WILDE BEUGER SOLMECKE**
	Don Spampinato	**Global Solutions Consultant - Digital and Business Transformation**
	Dr. Shermin Voshmgir	**Director Cryptoeconomics Institute at Vienna University of Economics, Founder Blockchain Hub Berlin**
	Katharina Zwielich	**Sustainable Fashion Expert**
Co–Authors	Amrei Andrasch	**Human Experience Designer and Creative Strategist**
	Jean-Philipp Almstedt	**Master Student in Cognitive Science**
	Victoria Balk	**Master Student in Psychology**

Co–Authors		
	Jannis Born	PhD Candidate in Cognitive Science University of Osnabrück
	Raquel Dischinger	Master Student in Sustainability Management
	Tina Dreisicke	Support for Change Maker and New Work Pioneers
	Dominik Frisch	Coach, Lecturer and Consultant
	Jukka Hilmola	Co-Founder at Soma
	Robin Jadkowski	Graduate Psychologist, Design Thinking Coach, Process Fascilitator
	Nimrod Lehavi	Co-Founder and CEO of Simplex
	Marcus Prosch	Brand Architect
	Long Qu	Corporate Trainer, Consultant, Ikigai Advocate
	Mats Richter	Data Scientist
	Friederike Rohde	Scientist at the Institute for Ecological Economy Research
	Stefan Pfeifer	IT-Consultant and Independent Author
	Romas Stukenberg	Co-Founder and Creativist at NAMENAME Creative Consultancy
	Maximilian Wächter	Product Development ACTUS GmbH
	Maximilian Weldert	Futurist, Sales Director Actus GmbH, Lecturer
	Magdalena Witty	Design Thinking Specialist
	Nicole Wohltran	Master Student in Business Education

Content

Text: Monika Smith

Do you know your why?

Your passion, your ambitions, your deepest motivation and desire? What is the reason you get up every morning and go to work? What are you uniquely good at? What does this world need? And do you know how to integrate and live that purpose in your business, your daily life, our future?

Purpose entrepreneurship not business romance. I'm talking about impactful, long-term, and human-centric business.

We live in a world where discontinuity, uncertainty, complexity, and ambiguity define our space and where entire markets, industries, departments, and specialist areas interact and correlate with each other. They do that in an unplanned and open-ended way.

We know that a holistic perspective over our society, the planet, evolving technologies, transforming economies and organizations enables us to understand what developments are happening and with what impact.

Still, most of us are stuck within our personal comfort zone, ignoring the rest instead of opening up for the reality. When everything is connected, we face a chaos of structured and unstructured information and an overload of possible scenarios. In order to take conscious decisions, orientation is key.

This is what the Business Purpose Design Model offers – a guidance for the most relevant topics of today with an outlook to tomorrow's world. Simple first steps towards a more purposeful entrepreneurship as well as a model to implement purpose entrepreneurship and create sustainable impact.

The Business Burpose Design Model defines six focus areas: Culture, Organization, Design, Commerce, Technology, and Planet. Within every focus area, the five most critical and relevant topics to generate impact are identified. Those topics make it possible to build a purpose balance scorecard for your company, project, department, or team. With it, you can measure the level of business purpose and its impact, and ensure a focus on impact-driven entrepreneurship. But be alert — purpose will only have a long term impact if it is truly integrated into the company's DNA and executed consequently.

Anyone who runs a business knows that the core challenge is building the team that embodies your company's culture and propels you forward. Creating meaningful jobs attracts world-class talents. This is crucial to create successful products and services that generate sustainable added value and secure your company for the short and long term.

I believe that in today's digitalized, connected world, our way of designing businesses shouldn't sacrifice positive impact — on the contrary, the two should be synonymous.

Lead Author <u>Monika Smith</u>

Monika Smith currently works as a Purpose to Impact coach, speaker and consultant for leaders, family offices and national and global enterprises. Being at the intersection of trends, technology, design and concept she brings new perspectives and methods to the companies and minds of today.

She facilitates change processes, challenges the status quo, highlights often unseen contexts between topics, and fosters purposeful, impact-driven and human centric entrepreneurship.

This is a co-creation project

This book offers a holistic approach for designing your business purpose, based on thirty topics in today's world for tomorrow. This cannot be done by simply presenting the opinions or expertise of one person. Instead, it has to draw on a multitude of cultures and perspectives to be significant and relevant.

For this reason, this book is a collective effort. For each chapter, I invited two to three experts to examine a single topic, looking at the status quo, recent research, and case studies, as well as drawing from their own expertise, to offer a glimpse into the future. Thirty-two specialists, from hackers to entrepreneurs, scientists to students, and consultants to coaches all share their experience in their respective areas in the section status and developments. After challenging the ideas presented in each and every article, we discussed the final outcomes and recorded our talks in the presence of two visual graphic recording artists. This is how the images were born, translating thoughts, ideas and complex information into pictures to make it more fun, playful, and easy to read.

I am grateful and thankful that such an excellent and truly diverse team made this project happen. Every one of them is a passionate expert, courageous and forward-thinking. I encourage you to have a look at their profiles at www.businesspurpose.design and not to hesitate to contact them if you need support in any of the areas covered by this book.

Who is this book for?

The book is for entrepreneurs, managers, lateral thinkers, change-makers, leaders around the globe and people who are curious about the future and open for new perspectives.

Reading tip

Don't try to read cover to cover. This book contains a lot of information based on deep research and many years of collective experience, and therefore it is not meant to be read only once. Instead, start with the topics that strike you as the most relevant or exciting. It's usually those that speak to you.

Scroll through the topics first. There you see the model on which this book is based, as well as the collection of 30 articles, one for every topic. The articles can be read independently of each other as they don't directly relate.

Each article follows the same structure and is divided into three sections. Section A Status presents an overview of the status, summing up where we stand today and offering an initial introduction to the topic. Section B Developments discusses current trends and challenges. Section c Take-aways offers you actionable thoughts and actions to start working on your business purpose and its implementation right away.

The yellow/grey marks serve as the crisp version of the book. By reading only the yellow marks, you should have an overview over all the topics in less than 42 minutes.

Please note that the articles don't aim at completeness. With our global and diverse team, we cover a good variety of detailed aspects, but our efforts are not exhaustive and never can be. Every company has multiple focus points and this can only be done by individual consulting and coaching. For more information, please visit the blog at www.business-purpose.com or get in touch with me at institute@businesspurpose.design.

Let's be present, and actively shape the world we want our kids to live in. Happy reading!

Business Purpose Design Model

In order to find, embrace, expand- and strengthen the businesses' purpose, the business purpose design model consists of five consecutive steps.

1   Train holistic thinking

Take a holistic view of your current and future business and its environment through reading and understanding the 30 topics of the business purpose design model.

2   Business purpose design self-test

After learning about the topics, apply them to your company by conducting a self-assessment test. With this test, you can compare departments, projects or teams on their awareness and future readiness regarding those most focal topics. Once the business purpose design model is applied, it shows clearly the areas where the company needs to focus on.

3   Identify yet undiscovered potential and vulnerabilities

Learn about the connections, dependencies and correlations of the different topics for your individual team, project or department. They can be then visualized and used for spotting innovation capabilities, potential weaknesses, or yet undiscovered strength. Furthermore, this knowledge supports the leadership in mentoring the teams and growing their potential.

4   Define and formulate your business purpose

Based on your learnings, immersing in the company culture and its vision, as well as reinforcing the relationship to the team, you can start formulating the business purpose statement. This differs from your mission and vision statements. The vision covers your values, the mission – the value. But the purpose goes beyond it, being the shared principle that drives the organization.

5   From purpose to sustainable impact

Once your business purpose is designed, the next step is to implement the purpose into your company's DNA and with it create an impact for its stakeholders. Be it the individual, the employees, suppliers and vendors as well as the society and our planet as whole. With the help of an impact balance score card, the impact level can be measured, controlled and compared.

Train holistic thinking

The business purpose design model focuses on six areas, which are Culture, Organization, Design, Commerce, Technology and Planet. Those are diagramed by the different colored circles. Within every area, five of the most time critical and relevant topics for impactful businesses are identified. These topics are universally valid for any type of company or project and are set for a period of six to twelve months. Then they need to get re-evaluated. The human being is always at the center, at the core of the model.

Why those six areas? Because they, as a whole, enable the most holistic view of human-centric entrepreneurship we need for our future-ready businesses and endeavors of all kind.

When setting up a company, there is a vision, a mission, and hopefully a purpose. And with it, a team that breathes the culture. Developing the culture further is only possible once the individual is present, and knows who he/she is, and where to belong. The organization keeps it all together, building the necessary structure to work in. Depending on its design, the way it is acting and creating products and services is crucial for its development. Making use and being aware of the latest technology is vital to be successful. Once the products/services and the pipeline to sell them is ready, the way how they are communicated and offered is in the spotlight, making sure not only the company but the system as a whole benefit. That means not only workers but also society and environment, our planet.

When developing the Business Purpose Design Model, my experience and research reached out to a multitude of other models. Ranging from Corporate Due-Diligence, Business Model Generation, Sustainability Certifications, Lean Start-Up Methodology, Agile Strategies, Integral Theory, and Systemic Coaching. I visited global conferences, exchanged thoughts with organizational experts, build companies the most holistic and present I could and out from that experience, sat down to sketch the first draft. With the goal to develop a model, that supports companies and projects to consciously and pro-actively do good while being profitable and staying authentic. I wanted to create a guideline, on how to develop a scalable form of purpose.

The six focus areas

The focus areas of the Business Purpose Design Model are diagramed by the different colored circles. Within every area, five of the most time critical and relevant topics for impactful businesses are identified. These topics are universally valid for any type of company or project and are set for a period of six to twelve months. Then they need to get reevaluated. The human being is always at the center, at the core of the model.

Culture

● **Planet**   ● **Organization**

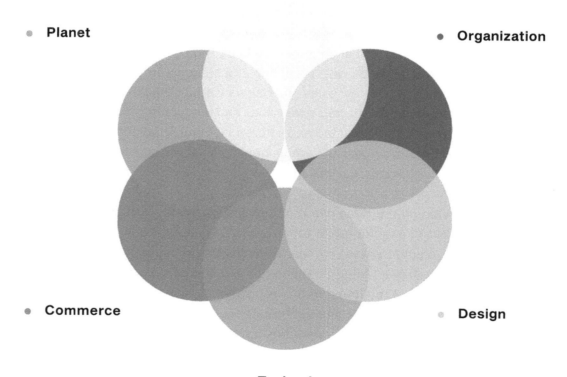

● **Commerce**   ● **Design**

● **Technology**

The six focus areas' ideal state

In an ideal state, all circles are overlapping, demonstrating the hyper-connectivity and unification of the six areas, displayed in one circle.

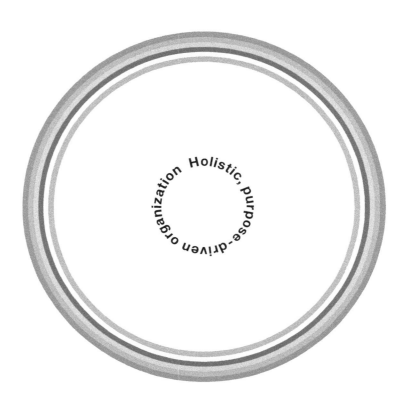

Step 2 Business Purpose Design Self-Test

After learning about the topics, apply them to your company by conducting a self-assessment test. With this test, you can compare departments, projects or teams on their awareness and future readiness regarding those most focal topics. Once the business purpose design model is applied, it shows clearly the areas, where your company needs to focus on.

Culture
Cultural Change

● Planet
Sustainable Entrepreneurship

● Commerce
Business Model Innovation

Organization

New Work

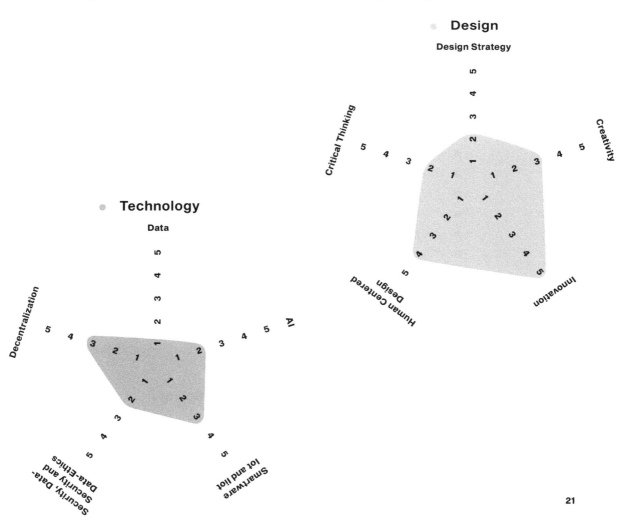

This is a sample result of the test. It shows that the company needs to pay most attention to the field of Technology and here especially to Data, Ai and Security related topics, as well as the to the field of Design, as there seem to be weak spots in Design Strategy and Critical Thinking. The remaining areas seem well implemented and but are still ready to be improved punctually. It is valuable to take the test on a team or department level and compare the individual results. Once you conducted the analysis, we develop a clear and workable action plan on which initiatives to take.

Design

Design Strategy

Technology

Data

Step 3 Identify yet undiscovered potential and vulnerabilities

By understanding the links between your company's most relevant topics, you can visualize the connections and dependencies within the areas. This highlights valuable insights leading to a broader understanding of the business, its prospects, its environment and weak spots. What you see here is one visual example, the applied model looks different for every company.

1	Cu	**Cultural Transformation** →S. 18
2	O ●	**Organizational Culture** →S. 67
3	D ●	**Design Strategy** →S. 82
4	T ●	**Security, Data Privacy and Data Ethics** →S. 141
5	Co ●	**E-Commerce** →S. 193
6	P ●	**Energy and Raw-Materials** →S. 207
7	P/Cu	**Critical Thinking** →S. 107
8	Co/O	**Leadership and Talent** →S. 62
9	O/D	**Organizational Structure** →S. 67
10	D/T	**Business Model Innovation** →S. 161
11	T/Co	**Payment Systems** →S. 177
12	Co/P	**Token Economy** →S. 167
13	Co/P/Cu	**Consumption and Growth Economy** →S. 219
14	P/Cu/O	**Well-Being and Inequality** →S. 225
15	Cu/O/D	**Innovation** →S. 95
16	O/D/T	**Innovation-Space** →S. 73
17	D/T/Co	**Human Centered Design** →S. 102
18	T/C/P	**Decentralization** →S. 151
19	T/Co/P/Cu	**Data** →S. 117
20	Co/P/Cu/O	**Production and Supply-Chain** →S. 213
21	P/Cu/O/D	**Diversity and Inclusion** →S. 43
22	Cu/O/D/T	**Creativity** →S. 89
23	O/D/T/Co	**AI** →S. 125
24	D/T/Co/P	**Smartware IoT and IIoT** →S. 135
25	D/T/Co/P/Cu	**Marketing** →S. 183
26	T/Co/P/Cu/O	**Identity** →S. 28
27	Co/P/Cu/O/D	**Knowledge-Based Society** →S. 31
28	P/Cu/O/D/T	**New Work** →S. 52
29	Cu/O/D/T/P	**Sustainable Entrepreneurship** →S. 201
30	O/D/T/Co/P	**Learning** →S. 37

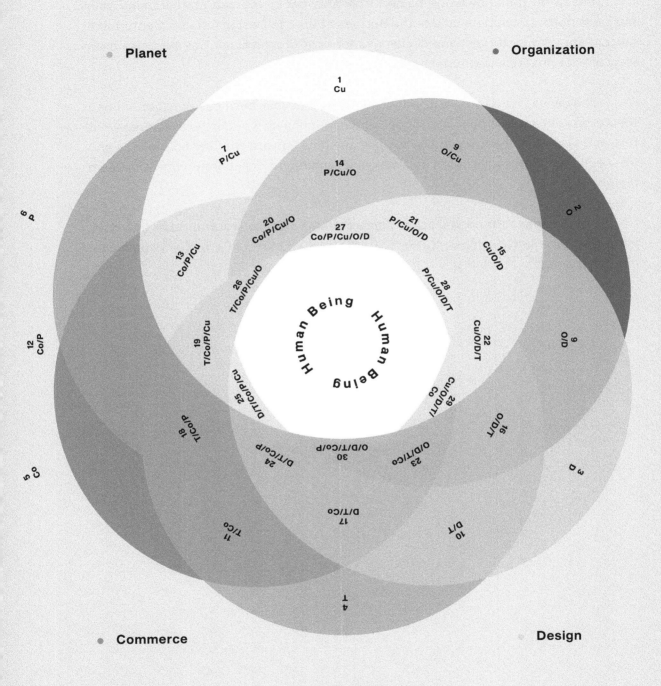

Culture

Planet

Organization

1
Cu

7
P/Cu

14
P/Cu/O

9
O/Cu

2
O

6
P

20
Co/P/Cu/O

27
Co/P/Cu/O/D

21
P/Cu/O/D

15
Cu/O/D

13
Co/P/Cu

26
T/Co/P/Cu/O

28
P/Cu/O/D/T

12
Co/P

19
T/Co/P/Cu

Human Being Human Being

22
Cu/O/D/T

9
O/D

25
D/T/Co/P/Cu

29
Cu/O/D/T/Co

16
O/D/T

5
Co

18
T/Co/P

24
D/T/Co/P

30
O/D/T/Co/P

23
O/D/T/Co

3
D

11
T/Co

17
D/T/Co

10
D/T

4
T

Commerce

Design

Technology

Step 4   Define and formulate your business purpose

Based on the knowledge gained from this book, you can start framing your business purpose with the help of the Business Purpose Design Canvas. Capture the current status quo, trends, and challenges for your organization. Get a precise overview of your drivers and future scenarios.

The canvas helps you to develop and formulate your business purpose, embed the Purpose in a viable business model, and continuously work on your company culture and evolution. It allows you to zoom in any time you are working on projects and (re-) building your organization and makes it tangible to collaborate with your team members.

The Business Purpose Design Canvas is sufficient to work through this book and create your first business purpose or validate your current Purpose. Go online for more resources.

Examples of purpose statements

There are many examples of purpose driven companies and entrepreneurs.

PepsiCo
Mission: "Our mission is to be the world's premier consumer products company focused on convenient foods and beverages."

Vision: "PepsiCo's responsibility is to continually improve all aspects of the world in which we operate — environment, social, economic — creating a better tomorrow than today."

Purpose: "PepsiCo is focused on delivering sustainable long-term growth while leaving a positive imprint on society and the environment — what we call Performance with Purpose. Our focus includes transforming our portfolio and offering healthier options while making our food system more sustainable and communities more prosperous. In doing so, we believe we will pave the way for PepsiCo's future growth and help others thrive."

Patagonia
"Build the best product, cause no unnecessary harm, use business to inspire and implement solutions to the environmental crisis."

soul bottles
"We want to work together in an appreciating way while also staying efficient. We want to be able to show ourselves as the people we are — everything included — but continue to take our tasks seriously and keep moving things forward. All of that, instead of having mentally already quit the job or constantly waiting for the weekend — no offence towards weekends.

We want to work together as honestly as soulbottles are plastic free (psst: 100% plastic free). And to express that honestly — as much as possible — free of judgement but with appreciation.

We don't want leadership to fall into the hands of a few individuals. We want everybody to be able to work in their area as autonomously and effectively as possible.

Clear and reliable processes make sure that suggested improvements — no matter who suggested them — turn into useful and tangible changes."

Business Purpose Design Canvas

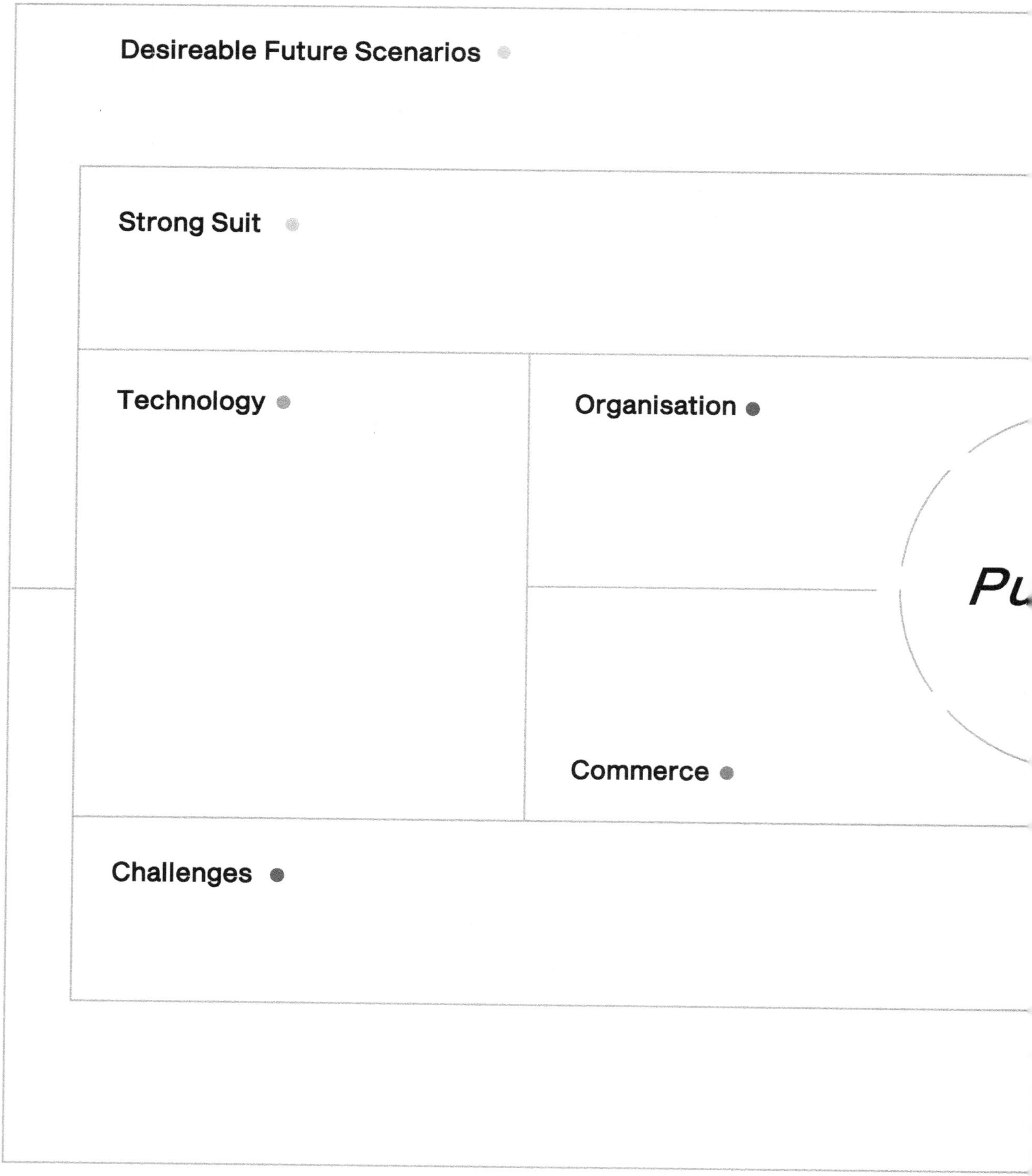

Desireable Future Scenarios ◦

Strong Suit ◦

Technology ●

Organisation ●

Pu

Commerce ●

Challenges ●

from

Shift

Design

Human

ose

Culture

Trends & Chances

Planet

How to use the Business Purpose Design Canvas

Start from the inside out – in the field of Purpose. Move on to the area of <Design>, <Culture>, <Organization>, and <Commerce>. Up next are the perspectives of our current state of <Technology> and us as <Human Beings> including our understanding of ethics, values and Social Responsibility. From there, you move on to the <Trends> and go over to the <Challenges>, and the <Planet>. It's time to take a short break. Open a window, take a sip of water, take a deep breath. Now you are ready for reflection. Fill in your organization's <Strong Suit>. What is your organization good at?

Then move to the <Shift> – and insert your change of perspective. Finally, you are ready for the <Future Scenarios>. Think of a time horizon of minimum of 10 years. Nearly there! Go back to the core, your < Purpose>, and formulate your Business Purpose. Ask yourself: "Why do we, as a company, have/want to exist?" Be sure that you align your business purpose statement with your team by including them in the creation and definition of your company's purpose and challenge it through your clients, employees and other well-chosen stakeholders. In general, focus on the most critical, strategic factors and don't aim at completeness.

Understanding Business Purpose

Purpose needs to be simple. Three ingredients define the power of Purpose.

Money
Money enables us to invest in ideas, build products, and develop our organization. It gives us the freedom to try out and improve, to get better every day and to have the necessary strength to produce, position, and sell our ideas and products – at scale.

Heart
Love makes the world go round. The saying is true as it can be. Empathy, humanity, compassion, respect for one another, and the ability to truly love are a prerequisite in any working culture.

Mind
To create an impact, we need a resilient strategy, logic thinking and different Perspectives. Therefore, a holistic view is indispensable. We need to understand the current status of the world, and it's challenges and possibilities. And a clear mind, to base our decisions upon.

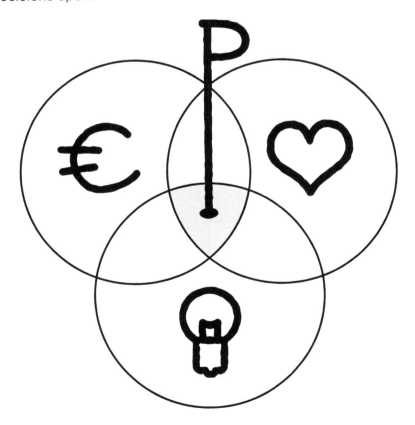

Step 5 From purpose to sustainable impact

Only if the purpose is integrated in the company's DNA, will it be lived by its employees and create the desired impact - on the individual, the customer or user, the employees, supplier and vendors as well as the society and planet as a whole.

Next step is the development of an impact scorecard.
With an impact scorecard you have the capability to:
- Track the initiatives you are taking to live your purpose statement
- Measure impact on your stakeholders
- Visualize the progress of your impact on a regular basis.
- Make this your framework for reporting your purpose driven efforts and results.

Impact Scorecard

Stakeholder Group	Objectives	Impact KPI's	Initiatives
Customer / User			
Employee / Team			
Vendor / Supplier			
Society			
Planet			

Objectives are high-level organizational goals based on your purpose for the relevant stakeholder.

Impact KPI's help you measure the level of impact and continuously improve its sustainability and strength, leadership needs to define a set of Purpose KPI's. Those are indicators that consist of key value drivers and goals which are relevant for the entire organization and its environment. The KPI's have to be easily comprehendible for the team and should be simple to measure and in their focus always human centric. You might have 1-2 KPI's per objective.

Initiatives are key action programs developed to achieve your objectives. Those can be Projects, Actions, or Tasks.

Upcoming

The whole is greater than the sum of its parts.

From here on, the book gives you an overview of the most relevant 30 topics for businesses, highlights recent developments and workable first steps towards a more holistic thinking.

After looking at the big picture through the lens of your company, you continue with Step II - Business Purpose Self-Assessment test. To continue working from here, it is strongly recommended to collaborate with purpose facilitators and coaches, who guide you and your team towards a purpose which really makes a difference in our world.

Culture

Intro

Text: Monika Smith

A business book that starts with culture? On purpose? That's right. Culture is the very foundation of humankind, the magic ingredient which holds us together, the anchor in times of upheaval and the place we gather to develop a sense of togetherness, love, appreciation, and trust.

From theatre, cinema, sport world cups, and the Olympics, to song contests, concerts, art weeks, music festivals, and regional cultural festivities like Oktoberfest, culture is and has always been the bedrock of human experience. It orients us as individuals within a nation, society, or organization.

"Culture, as the totality of the unique spiritual, material, intellectual and emotional aspects that characterize a society or social group, includes knowledge and artifacts, ideas and ideals, values and norms, as well as attitudes and opinions."[2] Through an appreciation of culture, we strengthen our humanistic values. Trusting our culture expresses confidence in the prospects and sustainability of society.[3]

Today, digitalization is everywhere, challenging not only our idea of work and leisure, but also fundamentally our definition of cultural belonging. As long-held rituals, rules, and language are being transformed, society is becoming mapped in a virtual reality, which has a huge influence on how we define identity. The sheer complexity and density of information can be overwhelming; tackling it requires the appropriate knowledge, education, and willingness to learn. Ideally, we will apply swarm intelligence to problems that cannot be solved by an individual, and by doing so, reduce the susceptibility to error. The more people have access to and exchange knowledge, the better. This potentially limitless information exchange opens up an exciting heterogeneity, a meshing together of different minds. Long self-evident, then, is the argument for equality and diversity. In this seemingly idealized world, humans no longer have to fit into the system, but finally find ourselves encouraged to develop our own identities. The paradigm is shifting.

To help you design your business purpose in the field of culture, this section includes chapters on Cultural Transformation, Identity, Knowledge Based Society, Learning, and Diversity and Inclusion.

I AM WORKING ON A SET OF FUNDAMENTAL VALUES

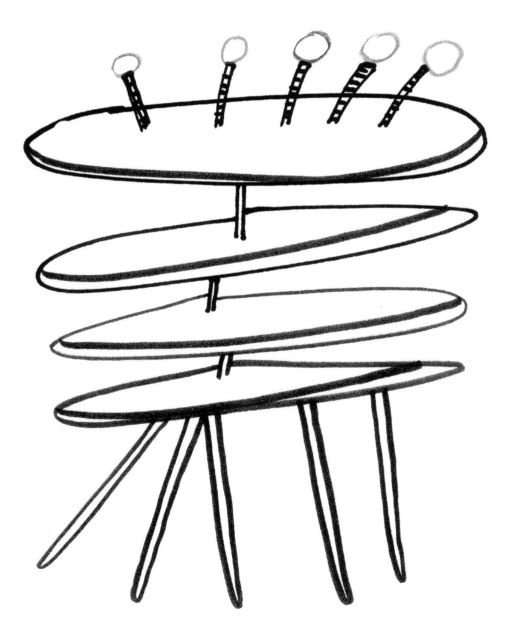

Culture

Chapter I

Cultural Transformation

Text: Monika Smith

A Status

The power of culture

"When we think of the world's future, we always mean the destination it will reach if it keeps going in the direction we can see it going now; it does not occur to us that its path is not a straight line but a curve, constantly changing direction," Ludwig Wittgenstein, Culture and Value, 1929.

Looking at our history, we see how powerful cultures can be. Approximately six thousand years ago, the Maya civilization, was the first known to develop astronomical systems and calendars even more accurate than the calendar we use today. They built cities which were combined to gigantic networks through roads. Or Ancient Egypt, a civilization in ancient North Africa dating back to 3000 BC. They are well known for their architecture, mathematical systems as well as their art. Those cultures were able to construct whole cities, be highly innovative and become very early pioneers of the society we live in today. How was this possible? Culture has the great power to unify people and not only organize their actions, but also motivate them in work. In the past, cultures were often nation based or tribal, they had one clear organizational system and set of rules and beliefs to follow. Information was simple and took time to travel. People could focus on their tasks and goals.

In recent years, the world has become complex, globally connected and fast paced. A chaotic – so it seems – environment that defines the pace of our daily life while our societal systems (politics, religion, education) – in their core structure – are still from the industrial age and are made for less complex and slower environments. This creates a tremendous imbalance between the old system and the new reality and also shakes up our beliefs, patterns and values. Jobs are not secure and the money the usual worker earns is not enough for paying high rents or saving for the future. The information we receive is overwhelming, biased and mostly targeted to our consumer behavior. We share more and more data via networks, web surfing, clicks and purchasing and become overly transparent and thus vulnerable to manipulation. This all happens because we humans tend to be lazy and trust our society and system to do its job. To care for us, to entertain us, to give us jobs with a meaningful task, to give us a role in society and be loved. These are all passive putting the human in a receiving position, waiting for it to happen, like the Maya and Egyptians did before. The big difference is that we can foresee what might happen; artificial intelligence takes over or we destroy our own environment with our constant "need" for growth and development.

In order to make a change, we need to step out of being passive and become an active part in shaping the world.

HYBRID
SOCIETY

Formation of movements

In the consciousness that our world has gained so much complexity through globalization and digitalization, more and more people wake up in uncertainty and with excessive demands. Some organize themselves in movements and get (pro-)active.

Times of upheaval are by nature high times for the formation of sub-cultures. One example is the swing sub-culture which came into place to show resistance against the political situation of the pre-second-world war and to demonstrate the joy and pleasure of life in uncertain periods. In more recent times, a myriad of niche cultures and movements have found space to coexist. People grouping together for environmental issues, humanitarian issues as well as for political direction and organizational topics, like in the seventies. All of those bound to one belief, one common orientation helping people to navigate their lives. And today, with all new communication channel and opportunities, we tend to believe it is enough to align virtually.

Usually a sub-culture, tribe or movement is organized around a vision and structured by a set of values, beliefs and principles. In software development, agility is one movement that clearly demonstrates how important values are. In order to orientate, seventeen visionaries agreed on a set of principles they called the "Agile Manifesto", which is now followed by millions of agile working practitioners around the globe, implementing that type of work into companies of any size. Another example is a global tribal movement called Burning Man, where 80,000 people meet once a year in the desert to build a city from scratch, and in the end burn the whole construction down leaving no trace behind – that means no trash, not even a tiny feather is left in the desert. Burning Man developed a set of 10 principles of human interaction with each other and our environment to navigate and strictly check that those are kept – for all their events around the world.

Another movement is the ban on disposable coffee cups, which is a movement that governments, companies and people are supporting alike. Many coffee chains are making pledges about how they plan to deal with the cup waste in the future and smaller shops and bars around the globe have already banned the one-use-only mugs to replace them with multiple use mugs. Scottish government buildings already banned disposable cups in June 2018.[4]

Looking at the growing movement of veganism, we see a subculture emerging with a huge impact on society, health, economy and agriculture. Be it because of animal protection, environmental issues, beliefs or health focus around 0.5 percent of the human population – or around 375 million people – are vegan.[5] The movement has developed a strong community around the vegan lifestyle, supported by movies like "Cowspiracy" and "An Inconvenient Truth" to vegan Instagram influencers. The movement created its own ecosystem, and major supermarket chains, brands and restaurants are joining in. Veganism has become a lifestyle, a community and a culture, based on the belief of being mindful and making a positive change.

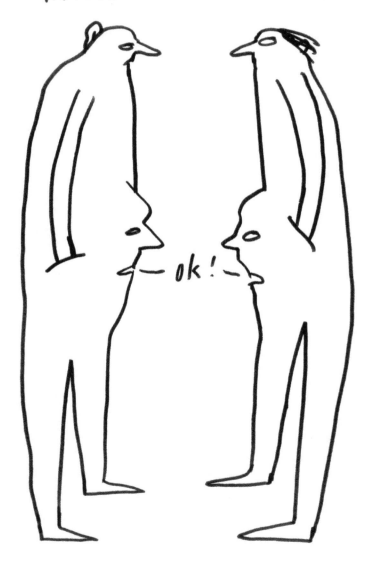

Focus on interpersonal discussions, allow time for discourse. This will lead to honest conversations that create a common basis of trust and strengthen your company's values and culture.

Values are an essential way to offer orientation. Make sure that your top company values are visible to – and can be experienced by – your team members and partners. Top down and bottom up. Examine the values that currently exist every 6 months in order to see if they are still lived in your business and valuable for your purpose design.

Hire a Chief Happiness Officer or Chief Culture Officer who helps to make your company culture more resilient and more successful. Being a top management position, the CHO works with your company culture, increases employee motivation and drives better performance.

I am a spongy
construction of things
that I am not.

Chapter II

Identity

Text: Stefan Pfeiffer, Monika Smith, Magdalena Witty

A Status

Humankind and machine

The Greeks knew the importance of self-identity — "Know thyself" was inscribed onto the Temple of Apollo at Delphi. The search for identity is as great a challenge today as it ever was. Humans have long been living in a self-created digital environment[6] so it's high time to consider technology in our identity-building. On the one hand, cultural pessimists depict a kind of burnout euphoria in which humans exploit themselves, where a rampant nihilism of youth is destroying us all. On the other hand, there is an everything-is-awesome society whose expectations for the future are no less fanatical, but rather too optimistic — kind of like Elon Musk meets Ray Kurzweil. During periods of upheaval throughout history and in our own time, it is common to experience this paradox. Which then begs the question: What is the digital upheaval doing to our sense of identity and our traditional understanding of power? How do we navigate online networks and establish our own sense of "self"? In the digital age, self-knowledge is more important than ever to keep us from drifting away in Facebook threads, Snapchat sequences, and fake news.

B Developments

Perception of us versus who we really are

A classic human tendency is to ask "What do others want of me?" and at the same time, "What do I want?" Previous generations' lived experiences were informed by clear religious or ideological dogmas and left little choice to the individual.

In our age of customization, we are able to present any image of ourselves we can think of, and that ability can be overwhelming.[7] How much are we really prepared to reveal? Self-determination is often confused with self-optimization,[8] and the two terms are not mutually exclusive. Self-determination in the digital age means being able to make informed choices. Self-optimization is an ongoing process of individual improvement, often motivated by the desire to please others.

"We" as a strategy for orientation

In the increasing complexity and flood of information that confronts us on a daily basis, others give us the opportunity to master this complexity. Why not view digitalization as a strategy to remain capable of acting in a world full of knowledge? As a set of tools and options to navigate and survive? The benefits lie in the focus on concentrated collaborative work, which is difficult in an ever-more complex environment.[9]

More time for self-reflection

Digitalization makes it difficult for us to take out time for self-reflection. There is a never-ending stream of entertainment waiting to engage us. At the same time, digitalization has also helped to make self-reflection possible, since we've gained more time through automation and industrialization. Our communication is more efficient, we live longer, and we're able to complete tasks more effectively and with more oversight. The ways we work now were unimaginable even twenty years ago, and in the next twenty years, this trend will only continue. If time is no longer a luxury, it's time to ask ourselves what we are here for.

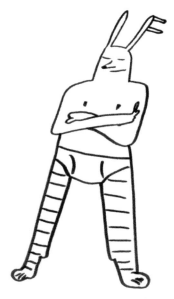

I FIND MY VALUE AT FACEBOOK.

THE VALUE EXPERT

c Take–aways   <u>Identity</u>

Find a comfortable, quiet place to sit. Now try taking a deep, slow breath. The air coming through your nose. Hold for three seconds, then breathe out through your mouth (or nose if that feels more natural) for three seconds. Then repeat this three times. Did something change in your perception of your body? You should feel more awake, energetic, focused and calm. Try to do this simple training every day once or twice.

You cannot start outside of yourself if you are working in the field of change. Find ways not to get lost in the infinity scrolling of Instagram, Facebook and other networks. Keeping a healthy skepticism about images, reactions and 'likes' helps to keep the scrolling time low and enables you to focus and use your time for yourself.

Find your purpose and if you already did, implement it into your daily life. Write down why you are remarkable, what defines you and how this can help you to create an impact.

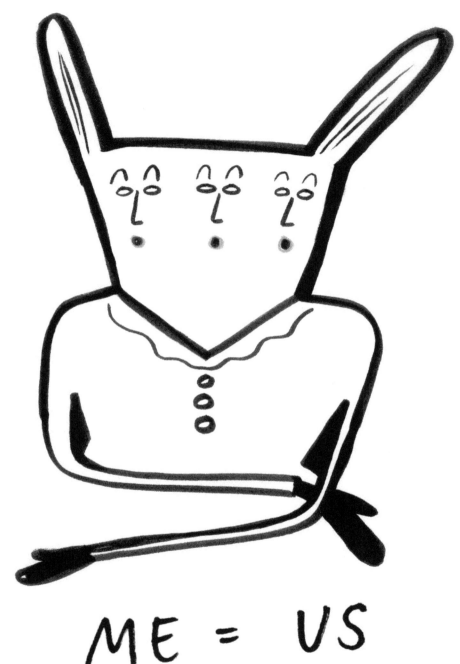

ME = US

Text: Jean-Philipp Almstedt, Monika Smith

A Status

Transition towards a knowledge-based society

Western societies spend more and more time on education, information and, brain work and far less of their time on manual work.[10] In addition to economic capital, knowledge has become an immensely important production factor for modern economies. We need knowledge as an integral part of (new) technologies and it plays a major role in the use of living labor force. Employees today are often no longer working in a culture of command and obedience, but of cooperation, as well as having a responsibility for processes and profitability.[11] Social knowledge plays a major role here, in a fundamental orientation of human action.[12]

Making knowledge accessible globally

Securing public access to knowledge, planning knowledge transfer, and building knowledge capacity in educational institutions are essential to drive change. Despite access to free knowledge via the Internet, we still can't boast a global knowledge society. At present, only the current economically dominating countries are really taken into account.[13] The mathematician and former CTO of IBM Germany, Gunter Dueck, believes that the old organization and the traditional way of handling knowledge and our access to it, do not succeed in enabling the individual to transform complexity into useful knowledge. There is a lack of an organizational culture in which talents, abilities and the search for good ideas can be nurtured. The basis of every community is personal responsibility – this is the job of the ego in us.[14]

Artificial Swarm Intelligence

A recent phenomenon is collective intelligence or swarm intelligence, where the intelligence of individuals is added together. A kind of 'super-mind', in which humanity and its networked computers have the potential to become efficient enough to be considered a 'superhuman intelligence'.[15]

Nature uses hive minds to tap into the diverse knowledge, intuition, experiences and instincts of groups and produces decisions that are better for the common good than being produced by any single individual. A swarm of honeybees, fishes or birds are examples of such a decision making process. And it is very similar to decision making by neurological brains.

Biologist Seeley puts it like this: "We will see that the 1.5 kilograms (3 pounds) of bees in a honeybee swarm, just like the 1.5 kilograms (3 pounds) of neurones in a human brain, achieve their collective wisdom by organizing themselves in such a way that even though each individual has limited information and limited intelligence, the group as a whole makes first-rate collective decisions."[16]

That Swarm Intelligence amplifies intelligence, is scientifically proven. Studies by the MIT Center for Collective Intelligence studies show that, even if the intelligence of an individual has an impact on team performance, the collective intelligence of the team plays an even bigger role. Especially in change processes.

The question is, can humans swarm? AI Professor and Entrepreneur, Louis Rosenberg answers this with a clear yes. He proposes using the global hive mind with a new technology called Artificial Swarm Intelligence. It's an opportunity to deal with the development of AI, to curate and control it, and to be able to fully understand it. He has shaped the idea of a human hive mind which works towards the greater good.[17]

It sounds foreboding, indeed the implications of developing super-intelligence would undoubtedly be immense.[18]

One example Rosenberg gives to prove his theory is the prediction of the Oscars. His team asked 50 regular movie fans to first predict as individuals the winner of the Oscars and then they asked the same people as a group to predict the Oscars. Worth to mention, that not a single participant had seen all the movies. They had all seen some of them. As a group of people the participants were able to fill the gaps in each other's information and converge on the best answer. The result: the individuals were on 44 percent accurate, the swarm up to 76 percent accurate, which is almost double the accuracy when working as a system. Interestingly, the professional movie critic was on average 64 percent accurate.[19] Due to our human, psychological nature, we function differently from computers, because decision-making processes run differently thanks to intuition or even emotions. We can therefore not only fill knowledge gaps but also make use of other signals we receive through emotions and intuition to enhance decision making. Human collective intuition is powerful, paired with the impact of AI it will be immense.

Filterbubbles

More recently we see an alarming trend in the notorious filterbubbles (search engines limiting their results based on pre-defined algorithms) and social media groups spreading conspiracy theories and hate speech. For critics of digitalization, this is evidence of the detrimental influence of alienated interpersonal communication that ultimately leads to division in society. The problem that closed groups eventually build up bogus realities is old.[20] Groups consciously decide where to stretch their limit in order to function and where to open doors in order not to slip into escapism.[21] Self-reliant individuals, formal or informal group leaders, and community managers need to be hyper-aware of the digital transformation and the importance of coexistence and intercommunication.

Create and establish a knowledge culture in the company. Create a central repository for knowledge. Give access to as many users and employees as possible and also share with your extended company network, for example suppliers. For that, use an online sharing system like Confluence (https://www.atlassian.com/software/confluence/knowledge-management-software) which is accessible 24/7 everywhere in the world.

Encourage various forms of knowledge sharing, taking into consideration the diversity of your team and their individuals skills. Not everyone likes to be in the spotlight, some feel more natural by better writing, others like to share links and documents and some prefer videos or podcasts. Make sure that you develop a knowledge sharing system that fits your organization.

Try to keep knowledge hoarding to a minimum. It occurs when one employee has knowledge that could be beneficial for the rest of the team, but does not share it for various reasons. This is more common than you might think and has negative effects on productivity and the knowledge culture. Design your office so that people can have meaningful conversations and are comfortable when having them. This could be the coffee station, your conference room and also common spaces like hallways. Make them comfortable and inviting by putting extra effort in their design, the furniture and space

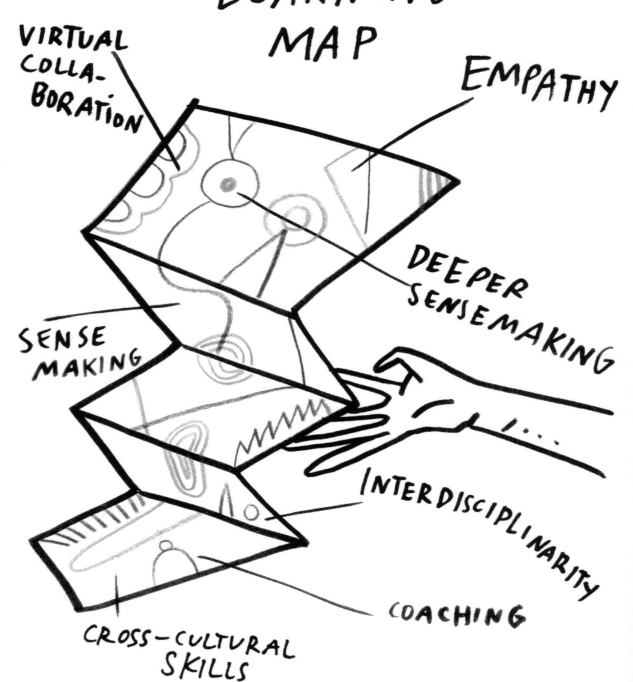

FUTURE LEARNING MAP

VIRTUAL COLLA-BORATION

EMPATHY

DEEPER SENSEMAKING

SENSE MAKING

INTERDISCIPLINARITY

COACHING

CROSS-CULTURAL SKILLS

Text: Monika Smith, Nicole Wohltran

A Status

To live is to learn

The process of learning not only involves gaining knowledge or absorbing new information, it also includes all behavioral changes that have their origin in experience. This is a constant and often unconscious process; with every perception, the network of nerves in the brain restructures itself and influences our approach to our current environment. Humans are genetically adapted to be good learners. The brain can only develop in interaction with the environment, and programs itself to exchange speech and identify faces. This builds on lifelong learning,[22] an ability that will be critical to personal, economic, and social success in Europe's knowledge-based society and economy of the future. That is why, even when we feel we are fully qualified for our jobs, it is important to keep learning and to develop innovative teaching and learning methods.

The social "us"

That fact that our brain can learn for a lifetime is a prerequisite for dealing with new things and situations, which is perfect for the times we are living in. Tanja Singer, Germany's leading neuroscientist, shows in her latest study, the ReSource project, that attention, body and self-awareness, healthy emotional regulation, self-care, empathy and compassion, as well as a sense of perspective, can be learned throughout one's life. This has implications for the workplace and the economic system, showing that a new kind of solidarity is possible.[23]

Interdisciplinary areas of knowledge

Our environment is increasingly intense and rapidly changing — economically, politically, and technologically.[24] As such, new interdisciplinary areas of knowledge and competence — including IT skills, foreign languages, technologies, entrepreneurship, and social skills — are rapidly gaining in importance.[25] Changes may be necessary due to environmental disasters, legal developments, new competitors, market disruptions, new technologies, dissatisfaction or new customer needs, or even an internal re-working of a corporate vision.[26] Various concepts such as change management, business process re-engineering, transformational leadership, and Kaizen/CIP assist organizations' change and learning processes. Organizational learning moves past simple survival strategies, to where individuals pool their knowledge to consciously improve efficiency and steer the company in a future-proof direction.[27]

B Developments

Changes in the educational system

Unsurprisingly, the education system is also undergoing radical changes worldwide, due to both the benefits of digitalization and rising demand for quality skilled workers in the field.

The share of digital solutions and content in the education market is currently only three percent, but will rise sharply in the future. Young companies, in particular, recognize this potential. Around 11,000 start-ups worldwide are working on "edu-tech" solutions such as IT-based training, training sessions and platforms, as well as digital solutions for managing learning programs and organizing teaching. New systems such as learning management systems (LMS) offer increased personalization in learning, including integrated online and classroom courses called blended learning, as well as flipped learning, wherein learners access content online, acquire that knowledge, and deepen it in the in-class lecture. Hyperlearning describes the massive increase in the use of new media to connect knowledge, experience, and human interest on a technological basis.

The importance of education is growing

Understandably, education is becoming more and more important in a knowledge-based society. The higher demands of the working world on social and personal competences require better educated (skilled) workers. Higher qualifications are in demand so that workers can keep pace with technological developments. Education is therefore regarded as a decisive prerequisite for modern economic management.[28]

New qualifications and skills are needed

The demand for highly qualified personnel will continue to increase. Reskilling, upskilling, and other lifelong learning concepts are needed. In addition to classical knowledge, there are a number of other skills that will determine personal career success in the future. These include sense-making, recognition of deeper meaning, intercultural competence, translation of data into abstract concepts, new media competences, transdisciplinarity, design mind-set, working memory management, and even virtual collaboration.

The democratization of skills

These days, much educational content can be completed online, meaning that people who didn't have the opportunity to complete a university degree now have access to advanced knowledge. Even professionals can equip themselves with particular digital skills that companies are urgently looking for. These include, for example, data science, machine learning, virtual reality, and robotics. A well-known example is Udacity, an online university that offers numerous courses and its own "nanodegrees." The aim is to make education available not only to a privileged few, but to as many people as possible.[29]

MOOCs — Massive Open Online Courses — are also gaining in importance in German-speaking countries. Established internationally, these online courses can be accessed from any location at any time. There are already a large number of users enrolled, and the subject areas are highly varied.[30]

New technologies enable new ways of learning

Virtual reality labs, such as those seen in aviation, have been in place for some time, but in the future VR learning tools will become much more widespread across many different fields. Immersion is a powerful tool for learning, and can be applied to countless scenarios. Users with controllers and virtual reality headsets

LEARNING BY EXPERIENCE

move within a small room, which, in combination with specialized software, feels like a real lab. VR is ideal for learning, as it combines experience with all sorts of data-driven information. Multiple users can also interact, promoting cooperation and collaboration; expensive or dangerous experiments can be carried out in a secure virtual space, and invisible processes can be illustrated.[31]

Within organizations, digital learning environments are increasingly being used for collaborative learning and work. A working group performs the tasks together, and then that knowledge and information can be shared between the individual learners.[32]

The possibilities for knowledge transfer are endless: Cloud and collaboration technologies make knowledge and information accessible across locations and departments, and increase employee productivity by promoting knowledge transfer and team collaboration. Employees and leaders can make their knowledge and skills accessible to everyone, thereby making the most of their existing knowledge potential.[33] We are now beginning to see tangible outcomes of machine learning as well, where new technologies make use of artificial intelligence (AI). Software giants such as Google, Apple, and IBM are attracting more and more start-ups and scientists to develop their deep learning expertise.[34] AI is being applied in driverless automobiles or for voice control of consumer appliances like smartphones, tablets, televisions, and hands-free phones. Computers will exponentially outpace human learning curves, the results of which are difficult to fathom.[35]

Enhance your organizational learning by sharing, collaborating and valuing individual talents and know-how. If you appreciate and understand your team's personalities and learning styles, you can encourage individuals to pick up new skills in a way that suits him or her. That might be a training, a subscription to a specific paper, specialist meet-ups to exchange the latest news and learn from others, or access to databases. Ask your team what educational opportunities they would like to have.

Make learning fun. In addition to formal education such as in-company training, public evening schools and private supplementary studies, the importance of informal education will increase. At the organizational level, you need to provide appropriate educational opportunities and recognition of informal learning. 54 percent of people learn on the job, through experience. This is why it is so important to create an environment that supports on-the-job learning.[36] Innovation bootcamps can help create innovative solutions while testing new ways of working together, skill sharing and making sure work gets done more efficiently or effectively.

Learn from mistakes. Conduct project reviews to find out what went well, what did not work out and what process will be changed to improve the outcome next time. Establish a culture of learning from mistakes, where it is rewarded to try out, to experience, to talk about it and to try again.

Text: Viktoria Balk, Monika Smith

A Status

Withstanding differences

According to sociologist Prof. Dr. Armin Nassehi, complexity and diversity stand for the ability to cope with differences: "There are many recombination possibilities, and numerous solutions; cultural and social. This is what makes the modern society superior. They always find a way. But that works only if we learn even better, to be able to withstand differences."[37]

Gender imbalance in leadership is still a problem

Equality of status, rights, and opportunities: As the American cultural anthropologist Margaret Mead put it: "Human diversity is a resource, not a handicap."[38] Anyone who wants to understand the new times, the new economy, and the new "us" must first understand and internalize this sentence. The world is moving away from traditional capitalist structures to the world of talent, where success depends on innovation.

In this world, equality at all levels results in the maximum potential. Part of this equality, of course, has to do with gender. The Global Gender Gap Report, which assesses the global status of gender equality in education, health, life expectancy, economic opportunity, and political participation, shows that although more and more women are part of the labor market, they are not distributed evenly across all levels. Rather, a gender imbalance persists in leadership positions: In 2017, Western Europe had a residual gap of 25 percent, although the economic gap was still well over 50 percent.[39]

In addition to legal innovations, there are now numerous movements, such as Sheryl Sandberg's Lean In[40] and the Berlin Community Female Future Force[41], which advocate for more women and diversity in leadership positions. They are committed to working towards gender equality, equal opportunity, and equal pay. Some of them also oppose the legally enforced women's quota and instead emphasize the awareness of gender inequities, supporting "more balance" instead of "more women." Their main objective is to achieve equal opportunities for both sexes.

Diversity in the working world has not yet been attained

In companies, diversity management often has a negative connotation, because there is rarely a clear idea about its benefits. It is evident that diversity management strategies are primarily concerned with reconciling work and family life, while neglecting other aspects such as the use of different talents, abilities, and ways of thinking.

Milagros Caiña Carreiro-Andree, board member of the BMW Group, in an interview with the Diversity Charter, states that diversity is successful when everyone sees different people bringing their strengths to a common goal as a source of enrichment, and when everyone is treated with openness, tolerance, and respect. However, it fails when it is perceived as a threat or disadvantage. In the company, it fails when the executives see no need for a change in culture, despite this perception.[42]

ONENESS is DANGEROUS.

Diversity management

Personality traits such as hypersensitivity and high intelligence are nothing new, but they are increasingly attracting attention. Recognizing these has become a part of successful diversity management. Initiatives such as Life at Work and B Corp (https://www.bcorporation.net) have made it their mission to support whole organizations or individuals on their path to authenticity.[43]

Increasing ability to act

In times of rapid change and complexity, challenges and tasks often require flexible and innovative solutions. Diversity favors finding these solutions, as it brings differing perspectives together.[44]

Digital participation in the context of universal values

Digital participation is the participation of all people in digital environments. This includes social participation, a key factor in one's quality of life. Many questions remain open: How an individual's use of the World Wide Web is influenced by participation, who is behind all of the algorithms, or even what happens to user data. Infrastructural emancipation in the digital field goes beyond empowerment as a form of competence and emphasizes the possibility to reflect on and evaluate one's own actions with digital technology.[45] After all, 193 states in the United Nations have committed to universal values and central principles of living together. To what extent do these values unite our society and our internal processes?

I ONLY CAN EXPRESS

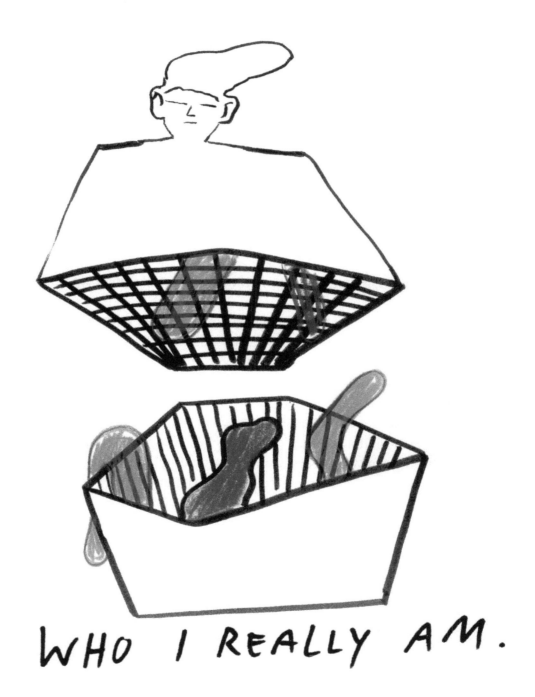

WHO I REALLY AM.

Start with yourself and drop any stereotypical thinking that is still left. Check the newspapers, blogs, channels, series, documentaries and podcasts you follow on a regular basis and make sure that those sources are balanced. Then work on your media and take time to follow news and people you would usually not follow.

Talk to one stranger a day. This will not only increase your communication skills, but also widen your horizon and network. Alternatively, invite someone random to join you for lunch.

Corporate cultures can be changed to allow people to reconcile their jobs with their non-professional obligations and other important events. This can also be crucial in HR processes, in competition for the best minds. Implement strategies to promote a diverse and empowered workforce. Create a culture of belonging to embrace inclusion in your organization on a daily basis. Share information, be open if an employee has an idea, a need or is willing to share.

Organization

Intro

Text: Monika Smith

Working to live or living to work — the question is outdated. Most of us these days aim to do both. Workers no longer simply rise up the ranks within a single company and retire on a comfortable pension. Indeed, the promise of this is rapidly fading. Both companies and employees now have to be agile; both must maneuver constantly in the job market to get the best result. The philosopher Frithjof Bergmann summed it up well back in the early 1980s when he advocated that employees look for work that has a purpose and suits their interests and passions. With his motto "Do what you really want!" the phrase "New Work" was born.

What is clear is that, in the twenty-first century, the age of digitalization, automation, and artificial intelligence (AI), the working world — and even the nature of work itself — is undergoing a major transformation. These are the perfect conditions for Generation Y, who are raising the questions of purpose and impact, sustainability and fairness, and contribution and transparency.

Employees are increasingly seeking out workplaces which better align with their own core values and where approaches to diversity and corporate social responsibility are actively engaged with. Employees want to feel comfortable to try out co-creative ways of working. This means that we need to re-think existing hierarchy structures and focus on our organizational culture including work environments.

To help you design your business purpose in the field of organization, this section includes chapters on New Work, Leadership and Talent, Organizational Structures, Organizational Culture, and Innovation Spaces.

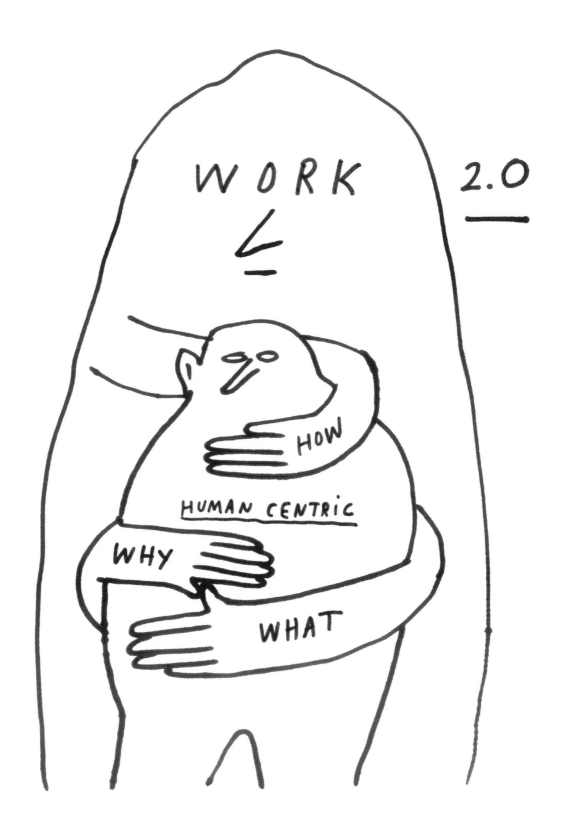

Text: **Robin Jadkowski, Monika Smith**

A Status

The transformation of the working world – New Work

"The mailbox was empty again today. Phone silent. No response to my job applications. [...] But I really have a lot to offer: Great organizational skills, I work well in a team, very good MS Office and English skills, SAP-R3 class completed with excellent results. I am hard-working and a fast learner":[46] So reads a letter to the newspaper Hamburger Abendblatt. Though published over ten years ago, the letter describes a situation still all too familiar to many people. They want to work – but they can't find a job. In Germany alone, more than five million people are looking for work or would like to increase their hours, according to the Federal Statistical Office. For many of us, our jobs shape our identity and define how others view us as people. Unemployment can feel like ostracization, and is often accompanied by feelings of shame and depression.

But it wasn't always this way: In ancient Greece, work was considered demeaning. It was seen as a mild illness, a hardship, something for slaves to carry out and suffer through. Free men did not have to work; as land owners, they had day laborers and slaves to work for them, enabling them to dedicate themselves to the more pleasant pursuits of philosophy, science and politics. It was only with the rise of the Christian faith that work came to be seen as something positive. Max Weber's Protestant Ethic describes work as an activity pleasing to God. Work was at the center of life; everything that was not work was "leisure." The German proverb "Work is work and schnapps is schnapps" sums up the mentality of the time: Professional life and free time are to be kept strictly separate.

The idea of "New Work" epitomizes the changes in the working world. Its creator, Frithjof Bergmann, defines New Work as, among other things, the need for a fundamental restructuring of the way we work to better deal with the realities of our time. Traditional reward systems, for example – such as wage raises, career advancement and job security – are increasingly ill-suited to twenty-first-century professions and working methods. Many companies have been slow to recognize this, and therefore risk losing their appeal among the younger generations of new employees.[47] Unlike their parents and grandparents, young people today are more likely to consider work as a valuable, but limited, part of their lives. They want to know why they are working and what they are working towards, and they want to a measure of freedom when deciding how and when to work. New Work thus represents the paradigm shift that sees workers not as cogs in a machine, but as free-thinking individuals who reflect on why and how they work.

The new guiding question: Why do people want to work?

"Work-life balance" was yesterday's concern. Today, the boundaries between work and personal life are so often blurred as to make the distinction all but irrelevant. Working hours – and even locations — are flexible. Given this new reality, we are now guided by questions like "How do we want to work?" and "Why would we want to work in industry 4.0?"

The new gig economy

Conventional nine-to-five jobs are no longer the norm; instead, new, flexible, project-based forms of labor now dominate an increasing number of sectors.[48] So-called digital day-laborers and self-employed freelancers work without benefits or fixed hours, jumping from one paid job to the next. These jobs are advertised on various online platforms that, to a certain extent, take the place of personal contacts and revise the classic employer/employee relationship. Many workers in the "gig economy" find jobs through services like Amazon Mechanical Turk, Helpling and Crowdworker, as well as Uber and Airbnb, which compete with traditional taxis and hotels, respectively, by providing transportation and accommodation.

Technology's transformation of work

Just as self-employment, flexibility and community engagement are shaping the way we work, technological developments like automation, AI and robotics are changing the kind of work we do. These developments have increased productivity, and although they have led some jobs to become obsolete, they have also created scores of new ones. Automation certainly seems to be the way of the future: According to McKinsey & Company, half of economic performance worldwide — equivalent to 1.3 billion jobs — can be automated by 2030. What this looks like in practice, however, will vary greatly from country to country, depending on the economic structures already in place, the complexity of the tasks to be automated, workers' average salaries, and so on. Right now, less than 5 percent of jobs can be automated completely; however, nearly every profession involves individual tasks that could be automated — and in 60 percent of professions, these tasks make up about a third of the work day. Digitalization and automation are the new reality.

AI technologies are poised to take on an ever greater role in many industries, and in the near future, it will be common for humans and AI to work hand in hand. This bright future may not be entirely without its victims, however: less qualified employees may struggle to make ends meet, provided that the demand for their expertise does not outweigh the automation in their field.[49]

An additional glimpse into the future of automated labor: MAN and DB Schenker are currently testing "networked, driverless truck convoys, which could soon make actual human drivers obsolete. The robot Hadrian is a one-man construction crew, able to erect an entire house frame in a matter of two days".[50]

Working world 4.0 requires different key competencies

The digital-age integration and consolidation of various types of work has brought with it a need for new skills. Workers must be constantly "upskilling," i.e. upgrading their qualifications, to keep up with the changing market. In addition to professional competence, they must also demonstrate a capacity for independent, synthetic, and critical thinking. Workers today must be lifelong learners — resilient, adaptable, resourceful, adept at problem-solving, entrepreneurially minded, creative and emotionally intelligent — to succeed in the new working world.

How can your company help to give an employee's work purpose? Remember that work based only on routine is monotonous, but work that stimulates the mind with collaboration, complexity, decision-making power, and learning experiences is intrinsically motivating and rewarding.[51] Allow space for development and trust your employees. When employees are given space to think up and implement their own ideas, they thrive; not only are they healthier and more productive, but their companies will also see lower turnover rates and higher customer satisfaction.[52]

Foster agility and flexibility at the workplaces by installing mobile gadgets instead of desk based systems. Make sure your internet connection is excellent in all the areas of the office so that your employees can work and take part in online conferences with good connection.

With intelligence and flexibility, the individual is an integral and indispensable element of the future-oriented company.[53] No company can grow without the ideas, creativity and commitment of its people.

LABOURTIME
is LIFETIME

FLATROOTR
love
FLAT HIERARCHIES

Text: Tina Dreisicke, Dominik Frisch, Robin Jadkowski, Monika Smith

A Status

Organizational structures lag behind technological developments

Digitalization has reformed everything from production processes to marketing and communication, yet the way people work within organizations has remained largely unchanged. The principles of scientific management, also known as Taylorism, still exert a significant influence on today's working world. The goal of Taylorism is to increase productivity through the division of labor; employees are motivated by monetary incentives and gain a sense of job satisfaction through the completion of regulated activities. But Taylorism, with its hierarchical structures, silo mentality, and reliance on control instead of trust, feels outdated in today's working environments. Our desire to reinvent our forms of work can therefore come into conflict both with social paradigms of work and personal belief systems. New forms of work challenge people to eliminate the boundaries between their professional and private lives and encourage them to fully commit themselves to their activities. Networks, creative freedom, decision-making power, participation and responsibility will shape the work of the future far more than the rigid efficiency of Taylorism. Yet current organizational models and existing paradigms cannot adapt to this new situation, and very few companies have made an effort to revamp their models and open up new ways of working together.

B Developments

Going beyond traditional organizational models

Confronted with the increasing irrelevance of traditional business structures, some companies have sought to implement alternative organizational models. Those are models like holacracy and sociocracy which promise to meet the needs of the employees and help them survive in the complex, global and digitalized world market. While some of these attempts have been promising, even serving as best-practice examples, there is at present not enough data to determine which methods of self-management have the greatest potential.

One feature alternative organizational models have in common is a high level of self-direction. This is covered by simple, consistent internal processes and principles so that managers can easily steer their teams through challenges as a captain steers a ship through a storm.[54] An overreliance on self-direction can, however, risk losing sight of the purpose of the work. To keep things in check, self-direction should be encouraged alongside self-determination.

There are many benefits to a self-determined approach: Self-determined and self-organized work result in shorter communication channels, greater investment in and identification with decisions, and efficiency in product development.[55] When every employee is responsible for themselves, every employee is a leader.[56]

Numerous alternative organization models also challenge the status quo in order to progress and collaborate. Through collaboration, competitive thinking is revolutionized: a competitor becomes a companion, management hierarchies are discarded.

In summary: future-oriented companies are methodically streamlined, largely self-organized, networked with other companies, and emphasize collaboration on vertical, diagonal and horizontal levels.[57]

New mind-sets requires trust

Implementing change in organizations is a complex undertaking. Developmental psychology has taught us that we are the sum of our experience;[58] in business terms, we might say that the organization makes the person.[59] Individual personality notwithstanding, an employee will behave differently within different corporate structures. So if we want employees to be able to adapt to and thrive in a new culture of work, we need to develop strategies to help them.[60] For an employee used to a more traditional corporate environment, the freedom of alternative structures can quickly become overwhelming. This risk is all the greater when employees are left to adjust to self-organization on their own, without proper skills or training. It takes time to get used to self-organization, and it only works within a pre-defined frame. At the same time, employees need to feel trusted and to know that there is room for failure. Trust nurtures security and creativity; when others trust us, we can more easily trust ourselves. With each individual employee's confidence in their own abilities comes a stronger team spirit. Solutions are formulated faster and more clearly when each individual has a sense of personal responsibility.

Trust also serves to help streamline agile companies. As long as New Work is taken as a serious guiding principle and not merely as a set of tools, trust becomes the foundation of a quick and flexible decision-making process. If employees know that they are guaranteed a degree of freedom in organizing their time and tasks, they are more likely to participate in discussions and decision-making. Transforming hierarchical industrial corporations into agile organizations allows them to better handle complex information; as a result, their employees are happier. A network of autonomous individuals efficiently managing a defined area on their own feels like a breath of fresh air in the dusty ranks of the old Taylorist companies.

GENERATION „Y"-LEADER COMES CLOSE TO THE „WHY".

While re-designing your organizational structure, bear in mind that not everyone is going to respond well to the change. Think about ways to get people on board by keeping them in the loop. And take into consideration that many people are not used to self-organization and an open company culture. Employees' expectations might change in the process of becoming more agile, so does the company culture. This can lead to conflicts.

Be the role model. Establish a culture of trust within your company and be transparent. In times of change and uncertainty, a good leader is needed to give orientation. Self-organized and agile working has to be approved and encouraged by the top level management.

There is no 'one size fits all' solution. Don't stick to rules that are not suitable for your company culture. Test and involve your employees. Create the new company culture together by including them in the process with a design sprint week or workshop.

ALL ARE PULLING.
IN THE SAME DIRECTIONS
↑???

Text: Long Qu, Monika Smith

A Status

Generation whY is changing our conception of leadership

Generation Y or Millennials grew up in a completely different world than Generation X and Baby Boomers. While Gen X and the Baby Boomers were influenced by a strong sense of propriety and collective values, Generation Y, as the first generation of digital natives, were exposed from a young age to an enormous wealth of information, social interaction, and controversy through the internet, social media and mobile devices. They live in the here and now and value freedom and private life. Societal and economic changes — shorter innovation cycles, increased competition, etc. — have required them to be more flexible than other generations, and they expect the same flexibility from their employers.[61]

Millennials not only ask how and what when it comes to their work, but also why. Meaning and purpose in their work matter to them as much as or more than money, and their understanding of leadership naturally reflects their values. Successful companies are sensitive to the complex demands of the new working environment and able to adapt to the mix of generations among their employees.

Many new terms have been coined to describe Generation Y's search for alternative forms of leadership, from authentic leadership to Zen leadership. More commonly circulating expressions, such as twenty-first-century leadership, new-era leadership, next-level leadership and post-heroic leadership, all "point to a re-orientation of qualities and values within management culture".[62]

How to attract, grow and keep talent

Talented people are essential to a company's growth — as long as their creativity is given room to play. Many companies make the mistake of trying to control their best employees or prevent them from leaving. They micro-manage them, set up unnecessary roadblocks and downplay their skills — all of which only serve to make employees feel frustrated and demotivated.

In fact, if a company wants to attract talent, it must do exactly the opposite. Good managers allow employees to be themselves; not only do they recognize and reward individual talents, but they also pay attention to their employees' personalities and skillsets. Each employee should have a task which suits them and at which they can excel. Just think about what a change it would be, if at least 80 percent of your employees do what they are best at, in favour of the company. For this reason, it is important that the work environment encourage employees to think outside of the box. If creativity is given free reign, both individual and structural obstacles can be removed: mental blocks can be overcome and restricting policies or structures can be changed.

Talent itself does not need to be managed; working conditions do. When conditions are kept flexible, the jobs of the individual employees can be altered and re-invented as needed. This is known as job design, and it entails proactively transforming and reshaping work.[63] This awareness of one's surroundings may sound like some sort of mindfulness exercise, but in fact it runs deeper than that. When the members of a team are truly responsive to each other, truly perceptive and in sync, they create a space for innovation and transformation.

Creating a good work environment

In order to work together well, it is important for us to pay attention to our own environment and the people in it — or, as the sociologist Hartmut Rosa says, to build up responsive relationships and willingly give up a part of our autonomy for the sake of group collaboration.[64]

B Developments

What makes a good leader

Good leaders challenge the status quo, implement improvements and follow through on their plans to create positive, lasting change. Leadership is not about competition: Leaders should not strive to be the best in general, but rather to be the best that they can be. If a leader lives by this philosophy and models it for their employees, everyone benefits, and everyone gets ahead.

As our expectations of work change, we are beginning to see our leaders as coaches, not bosses; mentors, not supervisors. We want leaders who lead by example, who encourage their employees and help them to become the best version of themselves. A leader doesn't even necessarily have to be a manager: Leadership in the modern business world takes many forms, and the best leaders are those who also know how to be followers. They are the ones who really understand where and how a group of people need to be led.

When employees identify with a company's goals and feel empowered by its philosophy, their creativity blossoms. A good leader not only has clear values and a guiding vision, but is also able to give strategic shape to their employees' ideas. By fostering an atmosphere of mutual trust and encouragement, excellent leaders can guide their employees through changes and innovations, inspiring dedication and commitment along the way.

Learning to coach

The leaders of the future will be coaches, not commanders. This seems simple enough, but many organizations, seeking to revamp their leadership styles, come up against a major hurdle: the utter lack of coaching skills among upper management.[65] Learning to become a good coach takes not only time and effort, but also a certain amount of maturity and self-awareness, and this is where things get difficult for many managers trained in more conventional methods.

Many managers, for instance, spend their days trapped in meetings as if in quicksand. Trapped in an endless cycle of giving orders and feedback, they accomplish very little of substance. Only by breaking free of these conventional routines are managers able to escape the pressure to justify their unproductive activities.[66] The key qualifications of the new working world will be results-oriented performance, integrity and honesty, and the ability to inspire and motivate employees. While it may seem challenging, these skills are the foundation of a culture of trust, and therefore essential to executive development.

Humble leadership

Humble leadership is relevant to an inclusive approach, since it combines empowerment strategies, altruism, and (self-)awareness. However, humility also requires professional competence attributed to leadership.[67]

Preparing for the shift to network-oriented, collaborative management

Good management offers employees the opportunity to cultivate a sense of meaning and satisfaction in their work. This truism is, however, often misunderstood in today's organizations, and attempts to implement it without careful thought can backfire dramatically. Without a sense of discipline, a participative, cooperative management style may fall victim to its own disorganization — an inability to keep deadlines, for example — or to interpersonal conflicts. On the other hand, when implemented well, a collaborative management style promotes self-determination and self-organization. If managers want to lead their employees to self-organization, they must first begin with themselves.[68] Managers should act as role models: "Instead of giving orders, they should inspire their employees and provide leadership and trust",[69] explains psychologist Peter Fischer. For a manager, asking the right questions is far more important than providing immediate answers.[70] Managing is increasingly envisioned as a way to empower others to assume responsibility, as well as a means of providing support for personal development. Ideal managers are servants as much as they are leaders: They are flexible, sensitive to the needs of their team and ready to adapt to changing conditions and requirements.[71] In light of this network-oriented, participative and collaborative approach, traditional, hierarchical communication styles feel more and more obsolete.[72]

GIVING A LEAP
OF FAITH

Stay authentic — it develops trust and respect between you and your colleagues. And showing a genuine passion for your work can inspire others.

Take five minutes to list your top three values. Being conscious about what you stand for puts you in a position of thought leadership. When you live those values consciously every day, you become a leader worth following.

Manage the working conditions, not the talents. Encourage your employees to think outside of the box. Start by doing this by yourself. Remember, job design happens on three levels: the task itself, the interpersonal cooperation between co-workers, and the larger attitude and approach towards work.

ICEBERG

MODEL

Organization

Text: Dominik Frisch, Monika Smith

A Status

Clearly defined core values make for a strong corporate culture

Good working conditions not only ensure employees' satisfaction and productivity; they are also a sign of a healthy corporate culture. Flexible working hours and fair compensation are not, however, enough to guarantee good conditions, nor are perks like fun evening events or weekend getaways. A healthy company environment is one in which employees feel confident in and proud of the quality of their work.

Clearly defined core values are essential to a strong corporate culture. A corporate culture is strong when its values are present and visible in the fabric of everyday life. Achieving this can sometimes be as straightforward as implementing and enforcing a few simple, yet effective rules to facilitate positive communication. If the company culture is one of listening actively, not interrupting, avoiding generalizations and preferring "I" statements to "you" accusations when voicing criticism, employees of all levels will feel respected, and concerns will be aired in a polite and constructive manner.

Visible and invisible aspects of culture

We're all familiar with the image of an iceberg: The small peak above the water conceals the immense mass below. In the 1970s, the American ethnologist and anthropologist Edward T. Hall developed a model of culture in analogy to the iceberg. In Hall's model, the tip of the iceberg represents the visible or tangible aspects of a culture, such as architecture or style of dress. The rest of the iceberg, the underwater mass, represents the invisible or intangible aspects: beliefs, motivations, expectations, etc. While an outsider can observe and easily interpret certain aspects of a culture, understanding what really shapes it, what makes it tick, is a more difficult matter.

Just like culture, communication can also be understood as an iceberg. The visible tip represents the actual contents of what we say: words, numbers, data and facts. But as we've all experienced, we communicate as much by what we don't say as what we do. The larger, invisible part of the iceberg therefore represents not only the non-verbal ways we communicate – including facial expressions, body language and tone of voice – but also the emotion or motivation behind what we say. Trouble on the invisible, relational level can have a negative effect on the factual level, so that an initially matter-of-fact conversation can be quickly derailed by an overly emotional, accusatory tone: "And what do YOU know?"

Interpersonal conflicts can therefore disrupt the practical aspects of work. In order to ensure good, clear communication, a company must hold onto its core values.

B Developments

A new management culture

Employees judge a company's corporate culture by the behavior of its leaders. If the leadership is full of drive and passionate about their job, their enthusiasm and motivation will rub off on the employees. The leadership will gain credibility in the eyes of their employees, who see their behavior and actions as honest and sincere.

A genuinely good corporate culture cannot be forced. No amount of slick PR campaigns or assertions of employee-oriented values or dynamic work settings will do a company any good if they do not really reflect its core values.

More and more companies are starting to pay attention to their core. The travel search engine Kayak is one example of many among modern companies: Habits are changing, especially at their Berlin office. There, you'll find no suits, no ties and everyone on a first-name basis — a marked departure from the traditional formality of German business culture. Flat hierarchies promote a culture of action; decisions are made more swiftly. Got a good idea? Go for it! What about meetings? Meetings are great — except for all those people. At Kayak, meetings were capped at three participants. The small size keeps everyone from wasting time and leads to a more effective group dynamic.[73]

Culture as competitive advantage

Performing well and doing your duty are not enough to achieve success; today, an attractive corporate culture is becoming more and more of a competitive advantage. In fact, it may make the difference between a good company and a great one.

If you scroll through job postings, you'll probably notice that almost every company boasts of its excellent corporate culture. But what is corporate culture? There's no single definition, and yet companies fiercely compete to outdo each other when it comes to it. As Simon Sagmeister writes, "Culture ensures the survival of businesses."[74] How can we understand what makes up a corporate culture? A number of analytical models have been developed to do precisely that. One of the first and best-known is Edgar H. Schein's three-level model, first developed in the 1980s. Composed of "artifacts" (tangible features such as furniture and dress code), "espoused values" (in mission statements and other official documents) and "assumptions" (largely unconscious behaviors and expectations), it is considered the foundation of all subsequent research into organizational cultures. In the early 1990s, Mary Jo Hatch expanded Schein's model to include a "symbolic" level. But in the end, all of the approaches that seek to describe or change corporate culture are based on the same principle: the ability to perceive and reflect.

Making culture measurable through cultural due diligence

All too often, one company will acquire another, only to discover that their two corporate cultures are completely incompatible. In order to ensure that integration — or even collaboration with a partner – goes smoothly, it is important to conduct a thorough evaluation of a company's culture. This is known as cultural due diligence. Aspects like executive management style, training and support programs, as well as compensation and company values should all be closely examined to identify possible conflicts. A careful cultural due diligence assessment facilitates a seamless M&A process and paves the way for the successful integration of two companies.

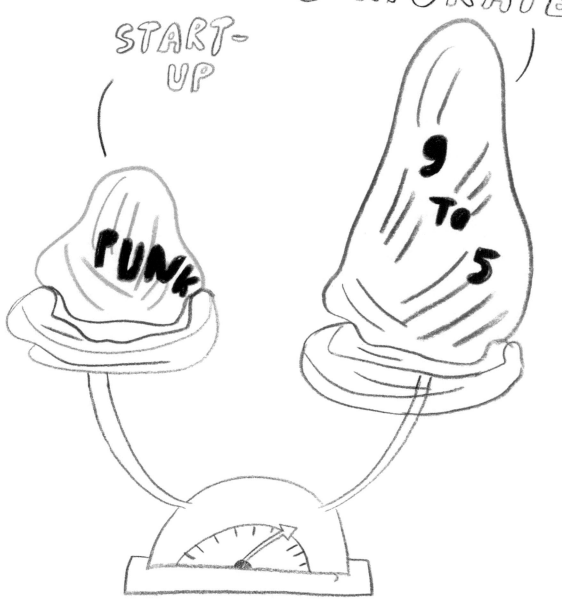

MEASUREMENT OF CORPORATE, BUT HOW?

Shaping culture

How does a corporate culture develop? Like all other forms of human culture, corporate culture is the result of both individual and collective behaviors. Certain whims of personality (motivations or skills), in combination with environmental factors (social obligations or expectations) develop over time into habits. When these habits are widely shared and condoned, a culture arises.

Creating a resilient organizational culture

Thanks to the dynamic markets and accelerated development cycles of our time, companies must constantly be dealing with change — and it's no wonder if this results in a certain amount of anxiety. It is more imperative than ever to create resilient organizational cultures that can weather whatever storms come and respond to new situations quickly and productively. A tough organizational culture is a competitive advantage. Resilient companies can handle the speed of the changing market without isolating themselves, absorb new trends and generate innovation without losing themselves in doubt and confusion.

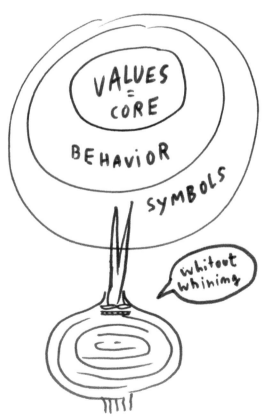

Ensure that your employees feel confident and proud of the quality of their work. Show interest in how they measure their own success.

Those who start a company usually have a vision, which is very much reflected in the company culture. Try to identify and communicate that vision clearly not only to upper management, but to the company as a whole – the culture will grow from there.

Start small, but do it now! That does not mean altering the corporate culture at the drop of a hat, but rather recognizing and developing situational or current cultural patterns. Start by building weekly rituals within your team.

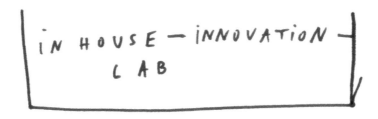

Text: Daniel Heltzel

A Status

Breaking free of ineffective and outdated behaviors

From meeting rooms and high-tech workshops to innospaces and innovation centers or labs — the relationship between space and innovation can take many different forms. Sometimes the connection is obvious, as when a concrete, physical room is offered as the location for innovation (as in a room or lab), while at other times, an abstract concept (such as space or hub) describes a space of possibility which facilitates creativity and development. In cutting-edge cities like Berlin, innovation spaces are as likely to be physical work environments as virtual ones. One thing is for sure: environment, work and actors — whether individuals, teams or entire organizations — mutually influence each other. This fact is key to effectively managing organizations; understanding the relationship between people, ideas and space is one way to break free of ineffectual and outdated behaviors.

Innovation Lab – do it right!

Traditionally structured companies often attempt to update their operations for the twenty-first century by creating innovation labs (or hubs or incubators – all three terms have become ubiquitous). Yet many never achieve any special success – why? In short, because decking out a chic office space with swings, 3D printers and kicker tables is not enough to stimulate genuine creativity. This practice, while admittedly very popular, is ultimately less likely to encourage innovation than to establish a cult. Those seeking to innovate should take note: an innovation space will not necessarily engender innovation.

Versatile working environments as a spatial equivalent to agile development

In some cases, however, a well-planned workspace can indeed facilitate innovative thinking. The most effective working environments are those that offer space both for concentrated, independent tasks and flexible, communal projects. These versatile spaces are the physical equivalent of agile development, which has extended to influence the business world far beyond start-ups. When designing an agile space, it is important to remain sensitive to the various needs of the company and its employees, and not to blindly follow current trends. Open-plan offices, for example, are no longer the be-all and end-all solution: individual, multi-person and open-plan offices, as well as free, unassigned work stations all have their purpose and place. These modern, mixed office concepts strike the right balance between individual and communal space, between privacy and concentration on the one hand and communication and collaboration on the other. Keep in mind, too, that these different spaces should allow for the easy use of both analogue and digital technology. As they move between different areas of the office, employees should be able to switch seamlessly from design thinking to flipcharts, or from working with 3D models and virtual reality to physical prototypes. Workspace planning is crucial, but while a good office layout can serve as a catalyst for good processes and decisions, it is not an end in itself, but only a means.

Curated co-working spaces as alternatives to in-house innovation labs

When looking at innovation and space, it's worth mentioning two examples of successful co-working service providers. Ansgar Oberholz and Tobias Kremkau (of St. Oberholz) and Christoph Fahle, Maximilian von der Ahé and Madeleine Gummer v. Mohl (Betahaus) are known as pioneers of the field in Germany. Their unique co-working spaces, both in Berlin, have served as inspiration to their fellow entrepreneurs for nearly a decade. At St. Oberholz and Betahaus, amenities include not only modern cuisine, but also community managers, who moderate the exchange between individuals, start-ups and established companies. In the best-case scenario, co-working can be a kind of matchmaking, leading to lasting and unexpected partnerships; in the worst case, things devolve into chaos and the system produces nothing of value. Working in close proximity, then, can be a blessing or a curse; it all depends on how people use the space. Even in co-working spaces explicitly geared toward exchange and collaboration, users may fall back into the old behaviors, working next to each other instead of with each other.

Conflicting goals in innovation labs:
driving innovation or changing culture?

Innovation labs are no longer merely a trend on the horizon; they are an important part of the modern business landscape. But what exactly is an innovation lab? Simply put, an innovation lab is a more or less independent unit within a larger organization, in which innovative projects are initiated and implemented. They are often intentionally kept separate, physically and otherwise, from the organization's established structures, including employees, processes and products. This isolation can be very productive: A well-run lab can produce unexpected innovations that lead to highly profitable ventures. But there may be a downside as well: sequestering the innovation lab can prevent the familiarity with and acceptance of agile work cultures from spreading throughout the company. If employees never have a chance to collaborate with the staff of the innovation lab, they cannot be experience and learn from agile processes. Following Silicon Valley's example, more and more German companies are establishing their own innovation labs – and failing. There are many reasons for this: digitalization is a company-wide task, and companies often struggle against high costs, low patience, and the challenges that come with isolating innovation labs from the rest of its operations. It is therefore key that management defines the innovation lab's goals realistically and strategically in order to maximize its efficacy. The lab's guiding questions must always be how, when, and at what cost new ideas can be launched, either on the market or within the organization itself.

Fab lab model for (connected) hardware

When it comes to designing and creating space for innovation, (connected) hardware often poses a unique challenge. Developing prototypes and final production models of a physical product requires money and room in a way that developing software does not. Traditional manufacturing companies generally do not offer ideal conditions for the implementation of agile, experimental prototyping, because they are configured for serial manufacturing and exclusive access. In the twenty-first century, however, in markets characterized by decreasing product life cycles, being able to create and test physical prototypes is vital. One promising model was designed to be an inclusive, accessible innovation lab for projects involving tangible products: fabrication laboratories, or fab labs for short. There are now over a thousand fab labs in the world, all based on the common principle of fair and open sharing of ideas and manufacturing equipment. The goal of a fab lab is to give as many users as possible the opportunity to turn their ideas into prototypes, while working together as a versatile community to find innovative solutions to current challenges. FabLab Berlin, for example, is physically and organizationally integrated into the innovation lab at Otto Bock, the world's leading smart prosthetics manufacturer. A team of scientists and medical engineers join freelance developers and start-ups to exchange knowledge and know-how on additive manufacturing (AM), among other topics.

The importance of coherent concepts

The enthusiasm for innovation labs certainly represents an opportunity, but it is not without its risks. The model may fall out of favor, or cause competences to become so scattered that labs lose their relevance. Decision-makers must be careful not to dive into the deep end without checking the temperature of the water: when constructing an innovation lab, location, partners and strategical goals must be chosen very carefully. Creating a new lab is not always the best option; an existing organization with an established culture might be a better and less expensive foundation on which to build a joint-venture innovation lab. The management's challenge is to develop a coherent concept that encompasses both a realistic approach to value creation as well as the corresponding KPIs and agile partners, such as start-ups. An innovation lab should only be assembled if a long ROI is acceptable, and if its effects on the company's corporate culture and/or public image can be assessed.

Collaborating networks of labs

Whether they are connected horizontally or vertically, labs drive innovation. Particularly promising projects can thus be scaled by making use of synergies between labs in different countries. A good example of a sensible, though still rather inefficient, horizontal network is the collaboration between fab labs: Because they are all structured on the same model, they can easily pursue collaborative projects. When it comes to scaling, however, a vertical network of innovation labs has more potential: Projects in specialized fields, such as last mile mobility, can be much more effectively scaled if similarly structured labs work in concert. The converse, on the other hand, leads to problems: it is more difficult to distinguish relevant from irrelevant — and therefore probably short-lived – labs in a vertical chain than in a horizontal network.

"Ever tried. Ever failed. No matter. Try again. Fail again. Fail Better," Samuel Beckett. Create room for failure and see it as an opportunity.

When creating an innovation lab, choose your location, partners and strategic goals very carefully.

Keep the work places pleasant and workable. Create a sense of responsibility for the work stations. If you have shared desks at your office spaces, this is especially important. Install a clean-up rule for the desks so that every team member is responsible for his work space. Ensure that there are enough possibilities for storing personal belongings and folders in lockers or shelves. And don't forget to check on the hygiene. Make it pleasant to share work space and offer desinfection and cleaning materials to use.

Learn from others. Lufthansa Innovation Hub (https://lh-innovationhub.de/en/) is one success story of the last decade. For Spatial Design have a look how the change consultancy theDive has created its own innovation loft (https://www.thedive.com/base1/) and how the Factory Berlin uses space and community to embrace innovation (https://factoryberlin.com). Connect with those businesses you feel appropriate reaching out to, to gain valuable insights into innovation practices.

Design

Intro

Text: Monika Smith

According to Nobel laureate Paul J. Crutzen, our planet has recently entered the Anthropocene era — the age of humankind — in which we have become the main factor influencing the changes on earth. In that sense, we now have a huge responsibility: We can determine the path for our planet. Our actions can no longer be thought of as independent from the effects of our human, laterally thinking mind. The discipline of design helps us to arrive at an understanding of this crucial relationship, allowing us to see on a macro level and to problem-solve from a humanistic point of view. The interactions between people, companies, and the world are crucial in this perspective. We become truly creative.

Design is experimental by nature, as it shifts the interactions both between people and ideas as well as between people and technologies. As such, creative disciplines have increasingly taken root in corporate management thinking. Design tests the future: What if, how could it work otherwise, what might be possible? The most innovative solutions emerge out of questions like these. The more it is in close exchange with other disciplines, the more powerful design becomes as an active driver of innovation.

From analog to digital and back — the entire universe of services and experiences are now being re-designed. The needs of people are once again becoming the key motivation for entrepreneurial efforts. The fact that companies' average lifespans are shrinking dramatically is only one of the reasons why self-questioning is becoming an increasingly important skill.[75]

To help you design your business purpose in the field of design, this section includes chapters on Design Strategy, Creativity, Innovation, Human-Centered Design, and Critical Thinking.

WITHOUT AN EXECUTIVE DESIGNER NOTHING WILL WORK

Text: Monika Smith, Romas Stukenberg

A Status

Design becomes central

There is a long tradition behind the use of design as an integral development tool. It began with the Bauhaus in Weimar in 1919 and was continued by Black Mountain College, founded in North Carolina in 1933. The core vision of both schools is social design — a bringing together of scientific, technical, and creative thinking, where humans and their needs are always at the center.

Today, many modern companies apply these skills adeptly. They shape corporate culture into social movements and package it with a clear message. One example is Airbnb, which positions itself as a social platform around the idea "belong anywhere." It is this type of social design which stands out and has become a benchmark not only for clever design thinking, but also disruption.

Design plays a role on three levels:

1   Creative cooperation. Design allows interdisciplinary cooperation within companies. You will learn how to turn complexity into clarity. Design also shows how creativity can be systematically applied to a problem and utilized most effectively by teams.

2   Sensitivity to human needs. Design can help you maximize the value a product brings to its users while highlighting the ways organizations can foster more meaningful relationships with people.

3   Mediation of socially humanistic ideas. By means of design, an entrepreneurial story can be carried into the world and the vision can be given a clear voice.

Strategic design is leadership competence

Companies serve people — not the other way around. Unfortunately, it is only now that we are rediscovering this banal insight and the humanistic achievements we have made. Fortunately, in the meantime, many companies and organizations have started this work.

Before we deal directly with human needs, we need to apply design thinking. Today, it is no longer just about aesthetic or ergonomic requirements. Much more fundamental are the social, emotional, and/or transactional needs each of us has. As a humanistic discipline, design today has a responsibility to promote a return to humanity within our companies.

Design processes benefit the company as a whole

By consistently applying design processes, designers can obtain varying feedback to improve the overall quality of the end product, in turn making it more successful. Why not open these design feedback circles to the whole company?[76] Design principles that are deeply integrated into the corporate culture offer businesses incredible value and a unique competitive advantage.[77]

B Developments

Activating creativity in leadership

More and more designers are being brought into management. The new title Chief Design Officer has recently emerged, with companies such as Apple, Pepsi-Co, and Johnson & Johnson hiring for such a role. The author Maria Giudice even speaks of the need for Design Executive Officers.[78]

Parallel to this development is the idea of STEAM. First conceptualized in the USA, it supplements the traditional technical courses of study — Science, Technology, Engineering, and Mathematics (STEM) — with the creative fields (STEM + Art = STEAM). The aim of this new approach is to promote culture within entrepreneurial innovation.[79]

In discussions on modern leadership, creativity has become a popular talking-point in recent years. The activation of the creative potential of employees and teams, as well as the consideration of intuitive knowledge in entrepreneurial decision-making, are increasingly regarded as management skills necessary to navigate companies through growing complexity and uncertainty.[80]

The customer's needs are key

Design is not just about beautiful surfaces or shiny pixels; design makes products work, so that they become invaluable for the end user. Florian Weiß, senior design manager at Deutsche Telekom AG, recognizes this:

"User-centeredness is the starting point for the entire design process. Technical feasibility and economic aspects only count later, because it is only worth innovating where there is a relevant customer need."[81]

This is undoubtedly the way to make better products — products that people need, want, and are willing to pay for.[82] By prioritizing design, we have a better chance of increasing customer satisfaction and loyalty, which ultimately means more success for the company.[83]

Design need not be scary

Design teams and creative thinkers in companies are experts in finding things you didn't know you were looking for. In retrospect, some would have preferred not to find something: for example if in the course of product development, the question arises as to whether the underlying business model of the company should be first modernized. Suddenly, the tasks become bigger than expected at the beginning of the project. In companies that are just beginning to embed design in their strategy, this can cause disruption and shock. Unfortunately, the reaction is often to impose control onto the design mechanisms, which makes the goal of becoming a design-led company less likely.

Pick up a copy of the book Digital Innovation Playbook by Dark Horse Innovation Berlin, and/or Sprint: How to Solve Big Problems and Test New Ideas in Just Five Days. These will help you get started with innovation methods. If you are looking for professional support, get in touch with our team and we'll find you the right person to help.

Open up a design position in your leadership team to help implement design-based ideas.[84] Don't forget to measure the effectiveness of your design. There is no one-size-fits-all approach; rather, each company needs to approach the problem in its own way and decide whether it needs this measurability in order to develop further.[85]

Try and embrace the different ideas that emerge as a result of opening up. You may encounter resistance due to the usual excuses of time and/or budget. Find ways to get people on board — creating small organizational design-led prototypes will help.[86]

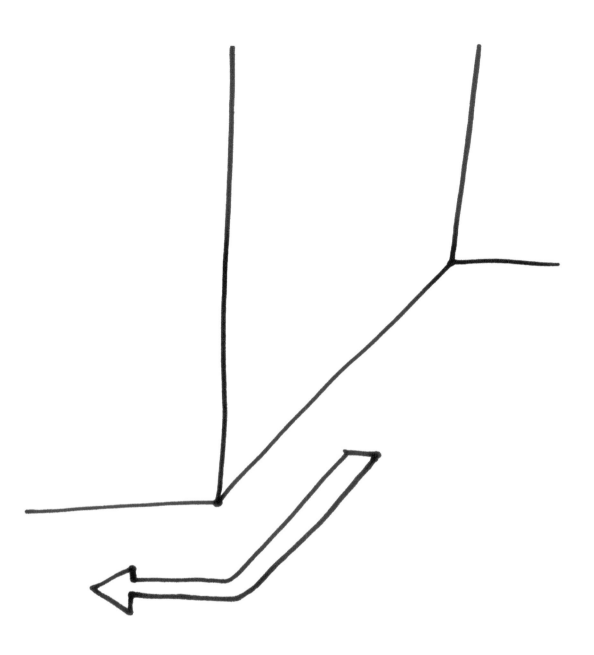

GUIDANCE THROUGH DESIGN.

Design

Text: Amrei Andrasch, Monika Smith

A Status

We are playing beings

According to sociologist Johan Huizinga, play is the basis of our rituals and myths, of our art and of our wisdom. And since our working life is intertwined with our social life, the boundary between work and play is increasingly disappearing.[87] This can be seen in the success of methods like design thinking, as well as in the widening use of agile techniques such as "Planning Poker," a game designed for agile teams. The game encourages healthy competition and play by challenging teams to estimate effort and development goals in software creation projects.

Schiller's famous statement that man is "only human when he plays" seems more relevant than ever in a highly networked world. The old concept of homo economicus is already obsolete — tomorrow's human is homo ludens, a player — as characterized in Huizinga's book of the same name. Playfulness is not a new phenomenon; on the contrary, it is one of the foundations of civilization.[88]

Curated games as a trigger for innovation

When we play, we open up space for creativity and try things out. We improvise, take on new roles, and imagine what would happen if we had new abilities or behaved differently. What doesn't work we throw away and reshape. We can play alone, go on a playful expedition in a group, or play against someone else. We can enter a playful dialogue with another person or team up to face a larger adversary. We learn by playing. Divergent thinking can make all the difference when trying to solve complex problems.

But not all games are just for fun. A serious approach while playing is highly productive. And whatever the outcome, the exercise is never pointless, but rather a valuable part of the process. A playful culture will do wonders for team morale: We feel safe in the knowledge our mistakes won't be punished, but instead, that our courage to take risks is supported. The journey into the unknown becomes less intimidating.

It's doubtful that as a society we would have ever discovered many new alternative futures without this act of play. For example, numerous moonshot projects of large companies work with playing methods, so-called "future projections."

As designers and thinkers, it's imperative to maintain a sense of spontaneity and open-ended curiosity about the things and systems we create. Those attributes come through innovation and play, not by returning to stock-standard approaches. Creativity is what sets us apart, and is absolutely indispensable in the innovation process.

B Developments

From play to creativity, the key qualification of the future

As traditional structures in companies disappear, people and companies must constantly adapt to new situations. This is an urgent call to update the rules.[89] According to World Economic Forum forecasts, creativity will become one of the top three most sought-after skills in the labor market by 2020.[90] That's because creativity can be described as an agile mindset, where the ability to rethink and reassemble things enables people to react particularly quickly to change.

Failure as part of learning

In a corporate culture where people have fun and perform at their best, creativity can lead to innovation. Balder Onarheim, professor at Denmark's Technical University in Lyngby near Copenhagen, sums it up when he says: "You can be creative without being innovative, but you can't be innovative without being creative."[91]

Companies and organizations that master a game culture often maintain a beginner's mindset: Those who do something for the first time are usually more willing to take risks and are not yet in a position to identify mistakes as such. By maintaining neutrality and staying alert, the biggest leaps in learning can materialize in a natural way. At some point in the process, failure inevitably occurs, but this can be accepted as learning within the context of the game.

Unlearning: conscious forgetting

"It ain't what you know that gets you into trouble. It's what you know for sure that just ain't so." — Mark Twain

Old beliefs, behaviors, or assumptions prevent people from developing themselves and realizing their full potential. In this age of Smart Everything and the relatively easy access to immense volumes of knowledge and data, we need to eliminate existing ways of thinking that can hinder problem-solving skills.

We are conditioned from a young age to perceive things in a certain way. When we find ourselves in a professional environment, these thoughts and approaches can seem immune to change. Unlearning teaches us how to think or act differently, how to deliberately discard obsolete, redundant knowledge that no longer applies either at the individual or organizational level. It is becoming particularly important for individuals, groups, and organizations to find ways to effectively support change, override old habits, challenge thoughts, overcome entrenched ways of thinking, and develop new ways of working together.

c Take—aways   <u>Creativity</u>

Have the courage to be strong, innovative, wild, and honest, stand up for your ideas. In everyday business life, this can take a lot of determination to swim against the current and deliver results that differ from expectations. Keep a good mixture of optimism and enthusiasm for your ideas to light up other's fire and win collaborators.

Enroll in an improvisational theater course. Improvisation teaches you to react quickly in unpredictable scenarios; above all, it helps you play in a way that is collaborative.

Challenge thoughts, concepts, and ideas. Do it even if it makes you uncomfortable to realize that something you once found to be true now fails to hold up. Unlearn and stay flexible to change your perspectives.

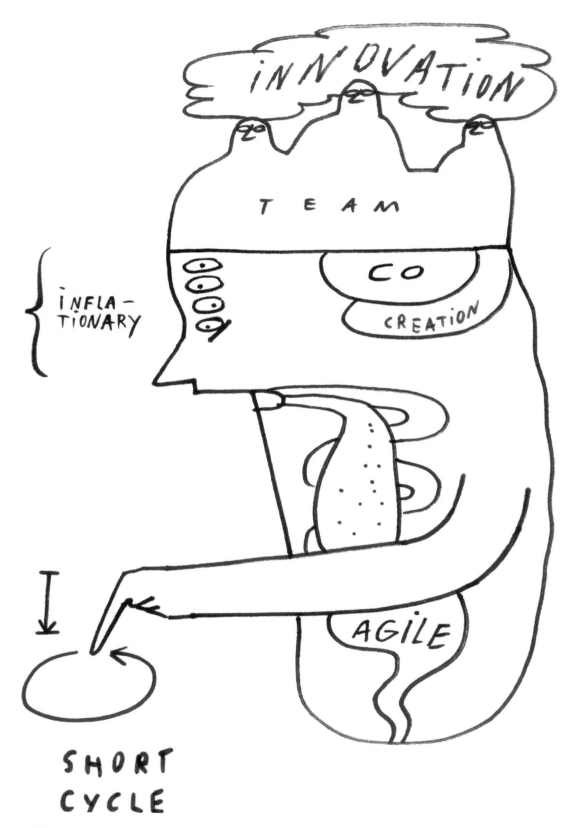

Text: **Daniel Heltzel, Monika Smith, Magdalena Witty**

A Status

Innovate now! A question of survival

Businesses don't have the luxury of time these days; driven by new technologies and a highly competitive market, they need to be able to react quickly. Companies that defend existing structures will run into trouble.[92] After all, organizational silos and risk aversion make cross-functional and creative cooperation comparatively rare.[93]

What is innovation?

The word innovation is overused. So what does it actually mean? Is it a ground-breaking invention like the iPhone, or a mechanical engineering company's customer-service app?[94]

"Innovations are undoubtedly qualitatively new products or processes that are 'noticeably' different from the previous state. This novelty must be noticed, must become conscious. The novelty is that purposes and means are linked in a previously unknown form. This combination has to prove itself on the market or in internal use. Simply bringing out the idea is not enough; selling or using it distinguishes innovation from invention — at least in retrospect,"[95] says economist Joseph Alois Schumpeter[96], who sees innovation as the critical driver of economic change.[97]

More than buzzwords

A manufacturing company that yesterday relied on serial production may be forced to introduce additive manufacturing (3D printing) tomorrow, due to high competitive pressure and in order to offer its products in an individualized form, i.e. with an added value. In order to initiate and control such changes, various management and innovation approaches were developed:

Agile and scrum teams help to develop flexibility, speed, and techniques for improvement, in order to react faster and stay ahead of the game. In an agile organization, information and data are digested more quickly, thereby increasing productivity is possible as well as cost savings and higher efficiency.

Design thinking supports teams by responding to the problems and needs of customers. With its build measure learning loop, lean start-up helps to find the most suitable solution for the problems identified.[98] Human-centric development approaches focus the company's activities on the decisive dimension —the customers.[99]

Agile approach speeds up development

Long development times still result in a bottleneck of rapid returns on investment from innovation and product development. In the BCG Global Innovation Study 2015, 42 percent of global innovation executives said that development times are too long. The same study shows that rapid innovations are far more successful and disruptive than slow innovations.[100]

A team that performs fast innovation acts like a start-up, operating with focus, speed, and agility. This creates the opportunity to bring a new climate of innovation to life.[101]

B Developments

Rapid prototyping

In close connection with the rampant "innovation fever," the accelerating development is not only economically effective, but also has an overarching effect: It confuses people's prevailing measures of time. Development times are getting shorter and shorter, products are not put in use for long before they are replaced, and innovative production processes are enabling fast production.[102]

If prototypes can be created quickly and easily, then innovation often increases exponentially.

Rapid prototyping — itself not a new phenomenon; it started with 3D CAD design in the 1980s — has expanded into potentially groundbreaking technologies such as 3D printing. As time goes by, costs will fall and efficiency will increase, opening these technologies up to ever more innovators. It's exciting to see how small start-ups could become like Airbus and develop totally new products on a much smaller scale, but with the same level of innovation.

To keep up with this rapid pace, it's helpful to have an open and dynamic innovation process in which prototypes can be developed and tested as quickly as possible. This requires a procedure that promotes iterations and is rich in feedback rounds. In this way, you can learn quickly from mistakes and generate new innovations through this constant learning.[103] One fact that is all too often ignored: Our absorption and processing speed as a human being is limited. This raises the question of the most sensible pace for both humans and processes.

Open and collaborative processes

Economies are currently being rethought and re-conceptualized. We need to move away from the isolation of linear processes in research silos towards open, collaborative, multi-stakeholder processes, in which not only the customer perspective comes into play at an early stage, but also the knowledge of other industries and disciplines.

Why shouldn't a big, blue-chip bank collaborate with a small but specialized fintech start-up? Sometimes innovative expertise can be found in the most surprising of places, which shows how start-up culture is shaking up the business landscape. Start-ups are small, agile, and in close proximity to one another. There is no tolerance for the isolated "island" approach. Systemic interactive models are replacing linear innovation ones. Collaborating companies can try out and disseminate new practices in an agile manner.[104]

Co-creation as open innovation

So where does the customer stand in all of this? They need to be the motivating factor; it's common sense — after all, "the customer is king." Customers are involved in product development because they know what they want, buy more and more on the basis of motivation, and support what they themselves help to shape. Professor Margaret J. Wheatley of Harvard University sees participation as an essential, self-creating principle of life.[105] Co-creation can be classified under the heading of open innovation. This means that the outside world is actively and strategically used to increase innovation potential.[106]

Teamwork fosters innovation

Research has shown that innovation can best be developed within groups and workshops rather than on an individual basis.[107] By focusing on a single task for a week during design, small, cross-functional teams can shorten the usual discussion cycle and reduce months of work to just a few days.[108]

Speed also results from the priority and focus that the participants put in when carrying out a task. A clear allocation of roles and incentive systems, as well as a dedicated innovation team with the task of acting quickly, are decisive for innovations and keeping the time-to-market short. The Boston Consulting Group (BCG) even reports that time-to-market can be minimized by a factor of four.[109]

R~~ABBI~~T RAPiD
PROTOTYPING

Design

Start Prototyping. Having big ideas needn't cost the earth. Simple prototypes — a storyline or a small model made of stapled cardboard – can often be enough to prove a workable idea.

Your most useful collaborator is sometimes the least obvious. Think beyond the usual members of your network, and get in touch with present and future customers, students, suppliers, and even competitors to solicit feedback.[110]

Be bold. Allow for the development of shocking, rebellious, or disruptive ideas that have game-changing potential. People have an incredible amount of untapped potential. Prepare employees for challenges that go far beyond their current job descriptions in the company.[111]

Text: Monika Smith, Amrei Andrasch

A Status

Yes, another meaningful buzzword: human-centered design (HCD).

Human-centered design is all about building empathy with the end user: generating tons of ideas; building a bunch of prototypes; sharing them; and eventually putting an innovative solution out into the world.

The HCD framework consists of four partially overlapping disciplines: user interface design, user experience design, experience design, and service design.

On top of all of that stands the human experience design, which supports the interaction and emotional connection between the product and the user. Through the conception and design of different models, new forms of working, learning, collaboration, human interaction, and innovation are made possible.

In order to tap into the emotional response of users, designers and engineers stage "experiences." These experiences, whether reactions or mental states,[112] help the designer to connect the product with customers and create feelings of loyalty, respect, and intimacy.[113] Service design is defined in close cooperation with companies and organizations in order to methodically develop customer and market-oriented services. User interface design designs the best possible user interface for machines, environments, rooms, and software. User interfaces now involve different senses: seeing, speaking, hearing, and feeling. Therefore, the user interface is directly related to the user experience, the experience a user has when using or interacting with software or a machine. This connection enables designers and users to go far beyond the user interface and design across devices and spaces.

Sensory overload!

An average smartphone user touches their phone around 2,617 times a day.[114] Different interactions call for different levels of concentration across different modes of engagement. According to the American endocrinologist Robert Lustig, the human brain is not designed for this level of multi-tasking. Multi-tasking creates a level of stress against which 97.5 percent of the population has no defense. Only 2.5 percent are "super taskers" — people with the unusual ability to do several things at once without increasing their stress level.[115]

It's up to designers to do more than "just" create the customer experience. Designers should take responsibility and become an integral part of the social discussion of future devices. What happens when AI, Blockchain, voice recognition, and AR are fully developed?[116]

B Developments

Screenless design and spatial computing

Human bodies are optimized for a world of space, weight, and distance. We have sophisticated spatiotemporal problem-solving skills, thanks to our ability to simultaneously connect the mind, body, and senses. However, modern computers reduce this rich repertoire to a mouse or a screen

New technical developments such as screenless design and spatial computing (dimensional movements, contextual scrolling, progressive disclosure and prototyping) offer further possibilities to integrate our body into the digitalized world.

With screenless design, our bodies and the world around us are merged into a kind of computer system in which we can rotate and optimize information with our hands.

By bringing computers, bodies, and space together, we can explore how spatial interaction design, i.e. spatial computing, creates future working areas and opens up new ways of creatively understanding the world. Perhaps we are now approaching what computer pioneer Bret Victor referred to as "knowledge work that integrates the body." [117]

Bots and conversational user interfaces (CUI)

Language assistants and chatbots have become an ideal first interface between a business and a user. The next step is conversational interfaces, which solve the problems of the user directly and across platforms. With their help, desktop PCs, smartphones, or devices can be connected and used without a screen, triggered instead by speech and movement. Apple HomePod, Amazon Alexa, Google Home, and Microsoft Cortana are all competing for market dominance in this area. In addition, devices such as Microsoft Kinect, Microsoft Surface, and Google Soli are evolving rapidly, making touch user interfaces (TUI) more suitable for everyday use.

Interfaces on demand

User interfaces that are only displayed when we need them — i.e. time-oriented interfaces according to the user's needs — make everything a medium for interaction design. In his 1991 essay "The Computer for the 21st Century," computer scientist Mark Weiser stated clearly that, "The most profound technologies are those that disappear. They weave themselves into the fabric of everyday life until they are indiscriminate."[118] One example from today's world are the voice assistants from Amazon, Google and Apple. They are integrated into our household appliances and are only asked for support if needed.

Maintain regular dialogue with your customers, whether it's through tried and tested formats like focus groups, or more experiential events where you can gauge responses with the help of modern technologies.

Add into your status meetings a regular review and update of your company's understanding of your users or clients. Don't be afraid to question your purpose and foster a critical ethic.

Stay in shape, physically and mentally. Only when you are in your best form can you create value for others.

IT

CAN'T COME
ANOTHER KANT.

A Status

Responsibility to reflect

Today as never before, companies have become the world's greatest creative force. Such power is also accompanied by a responsibility to reflect. Do we understand the effects of our actions? When our dreams and experiments mature into utopian ideas, it is time to ask critical questions and pause for a moment. This applies all the more to ambitious companies that want to change the world.

The role of art and criticism is often underestimated. Digitalization, driven by globalization, is progressing fast, sometimes too fast. There is a constant pressure to have power and success, to leave one's mark. The boundless internet has brought us closer together, but at the same time, growing nationalism is driving us further apart. Which discussions are useful, and which ones distract us from the important issues? The noise of endless polemic discussions shouldn't stop us from having real conversations — even unpleasant ones — in order to question and challenge preconceived ideas.[119]

History has taught us that every great euphoria is followed by sobriety, and that every shining new technology casts long shadows. Modern technology connects us to everything and everyone in the world and, at the same time, shields us from everything we do not want to hear, see, or understand. It's a dilemma unique to this moment in time.

A few years ago, the Dutch architecture and research office OMA/AMO looked into the subject of futurology. The key minds involved in this academic niche gathered statements about preconceived ideas of the future through crowdsourcing, such that those ideas could be historically assigned to persons and subject areas. It was then examined which statements proved to be true. Amazingly, the less people knew about the respective area, the more accurate their statements were. Operational blindness, epistemological communities, and the ball load of expert knowledge enable an interpolation of known knowledge. This can be misleading or restrictive when it comes to the future. Questioning, the applied principle of unlearning, the courage to debate and endure a high degree of ambivalence — all these are abilities that organizations must master, because they are increasingly relevant to success.

Escape the bubble

A kind of unanimousness has crept into our world — the desire for uniformity and orientation. We see it in people and their opinions, in user interface design, and in dialogue in closed groups and companies. Opinions are reinforced, and any other positions are drowned out. In recent research, there is the beautiful image of the bubble, which gives the impression of open and transparent structures on the outside, but no longer has a different opinion on the inside.[120] A society that can no longer tolerate friction stifles every hint of innovation. Our world needs discussions and cooperation between different stakeholders. Relationships and meaningful connections play a critical role in the workings of the economy and society. Without them, there is little relevance or meaning.[121]

Can design save the world?

In order to tackle the challenges we face, we need fundamental changes at all levels of our society. Climate change, loss of biodiversity, the finite nature of natural resources, and the growing gap between the rich and the poor are just some of the issues that require new problem-solving approaches. Transition design recognizes that we live in a transitional period where design plays a key role as translator, mediator, and critic. The link between social, economic, political, and natural systems must be determined.[122]

B Developments

The art of constant questioning

The world of VUCA (Volatility, Uncertainty, Complexity, Ambiguity) is disruptive. How can one be successful in an environment in which information has less and less prognostic significance, where basic conditions and motivations change quickly and constantly?

Leaders need a changed competence to establish a corporate culture in which the employees and they themselves feel enriched by change.[123] In times of permanent change, even self-evident matters are constantly put to the test. This means we need an agile culture with a systemic ability to constantly question.[124]

The ambiguity tolerance of the manager

The network researcher, Peter Kruse, advocates for a strategic shake-up within companies, by stimulating the types of conversations which alter our traditional cultural assumptions. In order to do this, managers need to create the right conditions that allow more personal responsibility, thus opening up important communication channels.[125]

Kruse talks about a 'third space' – one that does not exist physically but comes from personal interactions. And there can be any number of these. Managers should not fear complexity – by opening this up, people with different types of knowledge or from different backgrounds can meet and discuss context and meaning, adding valuable cultural insights to business practice. Since in the digital sphere much of this type of cultural information is missing, the importance of such discourse cannot be overstated. Beliefs, personal values, experiences and preconceived notions are thus the core property of this third space.[126]

Change in perspective

Corporate management is called upon to obtain information from an increasing number of perspectives. Anyone who is able to switch seamlessly and quickly between modes of thought becomes a valuable analyst of an increasingly complex world.

Such changes often include contradictions, such as the leap from a performance orientation (fast time) to critical questioning (slow time); from quantitative to qualitative thinking; or from rationality to intuition and back. These changes and nuances not only enable a faster and more effective handling of change, innovation, and growth, but also are a basis for purpose finding and design thinking.[127]

Sustainable design requires a radical change in our dealing with the world and the nature of our customer relationship

The design theorist Tony Fry introduced the term de-futuring, which refers to practices of modern, industrialized people who show little concern for the fragility of our future and environment. It is a fatal detachment from the effects of humankind's rapid progress. Sustainability does not only mean recycling and environmental protection; it is about maintaining our very existence.

Train yourself in critical thinking. Joining in a debate club, for example, will train your mind to think from viewpoints which you don't necessarily agree with. Without constructive and unpleasant discussions about the kind of future we want, we stand the risk of destroying centuries of progress due to our intolerance and isolationism.[128]

Challenge if the design of your products or services contributes to a future which is positive for people and the environment. Take responsibility. Think about ways to minimize the negative impacts they may have on the people who will use them now and in the future.

Satisfying a human need is not always the most important criterion for a decision, unless the definition of need includes sustainability.[129]

Technology

Text: Monika Smith

"My husband and I would joke and say I'd bet these devices are listening to what we're saying," said Danielle, who did not want us to use her last name. Every room in her family home was wired with Amazon devices to control heating, lighting, and security systems. Then, one day, Danielle received a phone call. "The person on the other line said, 'Unplug your Alexa devices right now,'" she said. "'You're being hacked.'" The caller was one of her husband's employees, calling from Seattle. Her device recorded a private conversation and sent it out to a random contact."[130]

What happened?

"Echo (Amazon's smart speaker) woke up due to a word in a background conversation sounding like 'Alexa,' then the subsequent conversation was heard as a 'send message' request. At which point, Alexa said out loud 'To whom?' At which point, the background conversation was interpreted as a name in the customer's contact list. Alexa then asked out loud, '[contact name], right?' Alexa then interpreted background conversation as 'right.' As unlikely as this string of events is, we are evaluating options to make this case even less likely," says Amazon.[131]

This is just one recent example of the current state of technology, in this case how error-prone voice assistants still are, and how people use and interact with them.

As data becomes the central component for control, we become more vulnerable. Machines will become increasingly autonomous and begin to think for themselves, even creating new human-like entities. When robots, automation, AI, and humans are all interconnected, how will we be able to maintain control of such a system? And do we have to? Topics like data security, privacy, and data ethics are becoming increasingly important and will shape future discussions.

Technology will solve many of our problems, and we will live even longer than we do now. Our daily lives will be more convenient and efficient: IoT products will be like butlers, taking care of our shopping, cleaning, and adjusting the lights in our households. As convenient as this is, too much is at stake to take a passive role in the way our future is shaped. Companies and organizations will have increased responsibility as they develop, test, and implement new systems like Blockchain and other technologies.

To help you design your business purpose in the field of technology, this section includes chapters on Data, AI, Smartware, Security, and Decentralization.

PURCHASED
A VINTAGE
DATA - BASE ?

Text: Mats Richter, Monika Smith

A Status

Big data: behavioral science is facing enormous changes

We are at a turning point in the history of humankind. Data is amassing in huge amounts, AI is getting smarter, and computational power is increasing. Soon, data will be behind everything we do, and today's currency-based markets will be replaced by data-rich markets.[132] Now more than ever before, businesses are converting this into a competitive edge.

Data is the new capital and is constantly growing. The International Data Corporation (IDC) estimates that in 2025, we will produce approximately 163 zettabytes of data — ten times as much data as was generated in 2016 (1 zettabyte equals one billion gigabytes).[133] One of the most important tasks facing companies today is to organize, understand, and find ways to effectively use this data for their own purposes. As Francis Bacon famously said: "Knowledge is power." Together with intelligent algorithms, data can be used to gain new insights that may help with decision-making processes and allow businesses to match their supply to the market's demands.

There are already many examples of these data-driven businesses in operation. One is the online carpool service BlaBlaCar, which brokers several million rides per month. Its platform allows users not only to select their ride by price, but also according to their preferences in drivers. A driver's profession or taste in music can play a big role in making a booking. It's no longer just about cost, but also about the overall experience, and that is where data can play a central role.

Data availability

The BlaBlaCar concept only works because the data is structured and saved in a manner that makes it analyzable later. However, many smaller or mid-size companies do not have that luxury. Important data is either not saved at all, or only in a very unstructured and inconsistent format. Organizing data can be extremely complex, but its significance is being recognized by more and more companies.

Large tech companies take the use of data several steps further. The online taxi service Uber attempts to predict ride distribution and utilization of the service by using metadata. IBM, Google, and Amazon are developing and optimizing mapping and other products on the basic principle of big data, while NASA is simplifying processes like searching moon maps for craters.

By constantly using even just our smartphones, we are creating a permanent data image of what's happening out in the world. When collected, this data can be used to identify behavioral patterns to make assessments about our lived environment.

The meaning of data

Data fuels our contemporary society. An interruption in the data stream would not only cause our companies to collapse, but also impact our daily lives considerably, both at home and at work. Applications, vehicles, wearables, and implants are increasingly controlled by data, according to the ICD 2017.[134]

Big data meets market research

Big data — that is, large amounts of data — allows us to gain valuable insights that would otherwise not be possible. With it, we can evaluate common patterns to predict immediate future behavior. Combining similar big-data analysis with conventional market research allows businesses to keep an eye on short and long-term customer needs. That potentially creates a solid base for a corporate structure.

B Developments

The mountain of data is constantly growing

Never before has there been a comparable amount of data available, and never before have we been able to extract this much valuable information from it. Businesses recognize this potential and are becoming increasingly eager to utilize their data to benefit their bottom line.

Analyzing consumer behavior in particular will become more and more important. Based on technological progress and globalization, products have a tendency to resemble each other. That makes them interchangeable. Placing more importance on marketing campaigns or creating well-designed service experiences can help tackle this problem. When these are done properly, they trigger the right emotive response and help differentiate a product or service from the rest.[135]

In the long run, companies will be able to devote more individual attention to their customers and their specific needs, particularly by automating complex production processes. The Internet of Things plays a crucial role in this development.

Moving data to the cloud

Collected data moves from consumer to business. As such, the information users save in social networks or apps automatically stays in the company's infrastructure.

Sorting out the chaos: clean, consistent, and complete data

Whenever new data is created, so are new challenges for businesses. Not all data is created equal in its importance, and not all of it is necessarily usable in its raw and unrelatable form. Successful companies will be able to separate relevant data from irrelevant data — and make it useful.[136]

Virtually every dataset contains a certain amount of inaccurate or incomplete data as a result of human error, defects, failure, or manipulation. In order for large amounts of data to be used effectively, they have to be clean and free from errors, as the term "clean data" indicates. Ideally, databases follow the three Cs: consistency, completeness, and correctness. Applying this concept to datasets from the very beginning and making them scalable is a huge challenge for every business working with data.

Mobile data access and real-time data

In 2025, 75 percent of the world's population are expected to have access to the internet. That includes groups of people that have not been connected so far, such as children, senior citizens, and people in emerging markets. This big jump in connections is going to produce all the more data. In 2025, nearly 20 percent of all collected data will be real-time. This creates a need for new technologies, so that data can be accessed in real time and with mobile devices.

Data security and ethical concerns

Ethical and legal concerns are growing at the same rate as the data mountain itself, and as such are becoming ever-more urgent. IoT providers are walking a fine line between providing individualized support and wanting to protect their customer's personal data. More data equals more vulnerability, for example when it comes to the theft of sensitive information.

Countless questions must still be addressed: What information gained from metadata may be utilized? Which data should be saved? Who owns the data? What are we authorized to use it for? These questions are elemental in today's society, because while data itself is neutral, the conclusions made based on that data are not. A connected car, for example, sends data to the dealer up to thirty times per hour. This information can be used by the manufacturer to continuously improve their product — but it can also be used to disable the charging feature on an electric vehicle if its owner has failed to make their latest payment.[137]

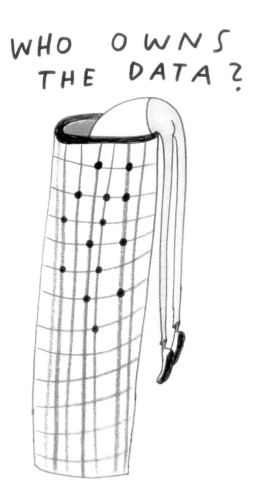

c Take–aways   <u>Data</u>

Treat data as one of your company's key values and assets. Apply the 3C rule (complete, consistent, correct) on all your company's data if possible to ensure data quality in all aspects and activities. Remember: decisions are made on data. The better the quality as more precise are the decisions. Sometimes starting with an empty database is more efficient than validating and cleaning existing data.

Think long term! Where do you get your data from? Is there bias in your data stacks? Which ones? When building a new product or service, maybe even building a new standard, using clean and fairly sourced data is one of the biggest challenges but also chances of today. The better is the enemy of the good – means constantly to benchmark and optimize your data sets and capabilities.

Get knowledge in-house by hiring Data Scientists, Data Analysts and Cognitive Scientists.

Try out virtual assistants like Alexa from Google or Siri from Apple to experience first hand how they use your data and what service they provide you with already today. Stay curious, but also make sure that the basics are covered and everyone has the same understanding (e.g. definition of terms or standard procedures).

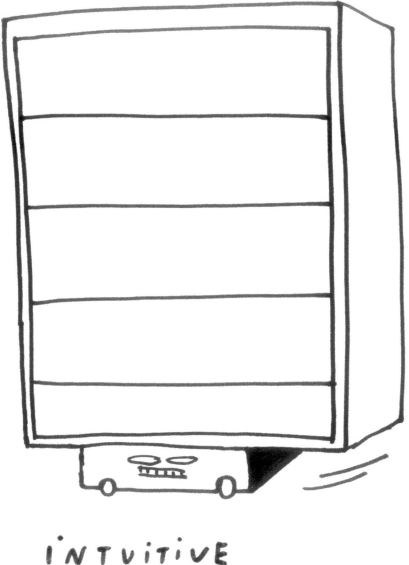

INTUITIVE
STORAGE

Text: Jannis Born, Monika Smith, Maximilian Wächter, Maximilian Weldert

A Status

AI is changing the world we live in

Machines take over tasks — or take them away, depending on who you ask. Just as mechanical weaving looms changed the industry in the 18th century, conveyor belts and assembly robots are shaping factory work today. Automation is not a recent phenomenon, especially in manufacturing. Now, however, technology has advanced to the point where automation has the potential to revolutionize all facets of our society. AI is penetrating every aspect of our personal and working lives: "AI is the new electricity," according to AI pioneer Andrew Ng, co-founder of Coursera, Google Brain and adjunct professor for Machine Learning at Stanford University.

Machines that learn — and beyond

By March 15, 2016, when the professional Go player Lee Sedol lost a match against AlphaGo, an algorithm developed by Google DeepMind, Artificial Intelligence became a hot and highly discussed topic.
While IBM's chess computer, DeepBlue, which defeated Garry Kasparov in 1997, was still a solely rule-based, hand-crafted device, AlphaGo learned to play Go all by itself through machine learning.
Whilst AI (Artificial Intelligence) is technically not a new concept, it had not significantly progressed in recent decades. Its origins date back to the 1940s, when McCulloch and Pitts developed the first artificial neutron model using Boolean logic and Alan Turing formulated the Turing test – a test to evaluate whether a machine's behavior is indistinguishable from human intelligence for an external observer. After the initial excitement, however, AI research stagnated. As Steven Pinker stated in 1994, "The main lesson of thirty-five years of AI research is that the hard problems are easy and the easy problems are hard."[138]
The key problem in creating a high-tech replica of the human brain is emulating seemingly simple skills, such as social skills, intuition, or consciousness. Finding a precise definition of AI is extremely difficult due to the thorny nature of the term "intelligence" itself. Larry Tesler came up with an implicit definition, later coi-

ned as the AI-effect: "Intelligence is whatever machines haven't done yet."[139] Outside of the science and tech communities, AI is often defined by a machine solving a problem in a manner that a human observer considers intelligent.[140]

Types of AI

There are two different types of AI: Specialized AI, also known as narrow or weak AI, is only capable of solving one specific problem. Generalized or strong AI, is able to overcome complex, diverse intellectual challenges equally as well as a human being could. Though the latter is certainly being explored in scientific research and development, for example by Google DeepMind or Numenta, it does not currently exist, and therefore does not yet have a significant effect on companies or individuals. For this reason, there are hardly any serious scientists or researchers who view AI as a threat to society's general welfare.[141]

Nevertheless, it is apparent that digitalization and automation will revolutionize the job market and corporate structures significantly in the next few decades.[142] For many purposes, specialized AI is sufficient, and it is already integrated into our daily lives: Apple's Siri and Amazon's Alexa order food for us online, IBM's Watson is replacing insurance jobs in Japan, and self-driving cars are on the way to cruising through our major cities.

Machine learning

The main goal of machine learning (ML) is to make predictions based on statistical inferences. Most commercially applied AI systems are based on ML, particularly on and so-called neural networks (NN). The two most important success stories from the last decade of research are the training of deep neural networks (deep learning)[143] and the development of generative neural networks (GAN).[144]

In practice, deep learning is implemented through intensive computation with on powerful processors, often parallelized graphic processors (GPUs), on cloud computing services like Amazon Web Services (AWS). Many AI applications are programmed with Python-based libraries such as Theano, Torch, Caffe, and especially Google's TensorFlow, which quickly claimed a leading market position after its first release in late 2015.

By demanding intuitive decisions, generative neural networks realized certain previously unattainable applications. A perfect example is a model that can warp a photograph into the style of a famous painter, or that can take a pixelated photo and reconstruct the high-resolution original. For both tasks, the AI has to be able to read and in a sense understand the photograph, which until very recently was something only humans were able to do.

Machines are currently not able to emulate the emotional part of human intelligence or to exhibit empathy. An important part of our organic intelligence is "embodied consciousness," which AI is not (yet) able to reproduce. AI still lacks dreams, visions, and the exchange of needs based on an ethical understanding.

B Developments

The market is growing

The frequency of the term "artificial intelligence" in journals increased annually between 2014 and 2017 — and in 2016 it surpassed "big data." The US market research institute Tractica estimates that the worldwide profit made by AI, currently at US $644 million, is likely to grow to approximately $37 billion by 2025. That is a yearly growth rate of nearly 57 percent.[145] Key players in the tech world invested between $20 – 30 billion into the AI sector in 2016 alone. Ninety percent of those investments were allocated to development, and only 10 percent went into the acquisition of start-ups.[146] The areas that stood out the most were machine learning and computer vision.[147] The key to growth is innovation: The Big Five (Google, Facebook, Microsoft, Apple, Amazon) increased the amount of AI patents sevenfold between 2009 and 2014.[148]

Added value through AI

Long-lasting studies of AI's efficiency do not yet exist. In fact, AI's effects on the economy have never been measured. But one thing is clear: Businesses that integrate or develop AI early on have an advantage. Companies that choose to pursue a digitally oriented mindset are able to adapt more quickly, and have a better chance of survival in the long term. Their profit margins are typically higher, and they have an obvious competitive advantage over more traditional corporations.[149]

Examples are plentiful: Online marketplaces work with AI-controlled robots that are capable of fulfilling logistical tasks and stocking their warehouses as efficiently and cost effectively as possible. Doctors use AI to screen cancer or sequence DNA. Some technologies are able to diagnose conditions more quickly and reliably than any human doctor, and others can even suggest individual treatment plans.

The rise of the tech giants

Traditional companies now find themselves in direct competition with global tech leaders that continuously expand in seemingly stable markets. Global players are known to either develop the necessary AI technology in-house, or take over specialized start-up companies (over 200 acquisitions have been recorded since 2012, most of them by Google).[150]

Amazon Prime Air, for example, competes directly with well-established package-delivery services. In order to considerably speed up the delivery process, Amazon purchased the robotics company Kiva for $775 million: A product now leaves the logistics center a mere fifteen minutes after purchase has been completed. Human order-processing, by contrast, would take between sixty and seventy-five minutes. As a welcome side effect, the maintenance cost decreased by 20 percent and the warehouse capacity increased by 50 percent.[151]

Turning AI into a real-world solution

This is a challenge every company will face. Similar to the way electricity revolutionized existing industries and created new ones, AI has the power to drive the development of entire sectors. While businesses with increased technical affinity, such as high-tech companies in telecommunications, finance, or retail, have natural advantages in accomplishing upcoming challenges, sectors like tourism, construction or education are less experienced in AI nowadays and will not reap the same benefits from it.

In order to stay competitive, for companies in these sectors need to implement AI applications in the long run. This may happen through new technologies that are capable of solving industry-specific problems, or through training an interdisciplinary workforce that acts as a connection between AI and more traditional areas of the business. One example of this dynamic are decentralized marketplaces such as SingularityNET.[152]

Ethical technology

AI poses new questions. For the first time, we are allowing machines to make decisions, not based on a set of rules defined by a developer, but rather on their own. Self-driving cars are an extreme example: There will be unsatisfactory decisions, to put it mildly.[153] Programmers carry the responsibility of implementing an ethical code into the vehicles, which, in extreme cases, decides about life or death. While there is hope that 90 percent of today's accidents could be avoided through AI, many ethical dilemmas still remain unresolved.[154]

Questions of ethics and responsibility are also emerging in relation to other AI applications. When algorithms are expected to learn on their own, they typically learn from humans. It is our responsibility to teach them the right thing. "Be nice to robots" could become an important rule of etiquette for the future.

The good news: More and more people are facing these ethical decisions. That is crucial in order to solve questions of responsibility before they become acute.[155] It is society's duty to debate the countless unsolved ethical issues and create a legal environment in which AI technology can flourish and progress, while at the same time ensuring that our privacy is protected — even if we need to redefine what that means.

Data quality and availability

The quality of AI usually depends on the quality of the data. In many large corporations, however, the data quality leaves a lot to be desired. It is either incomplete, or only available in fragmented digital form. Furthermore, there are no standards when it comes to AI documentation practices, which makes standardized control impossible.[156]

Building trust in AI

AI can only be established if people trust its decisions. Building this kind of trust is a real challenge. Even now, more people than ever believe that AI may have a very negative impact on humankind's future. Many detractors possibly overlook the aforementioned difference between narrow AI and generalized AI (AGI).

Nevertheless, the establishment of AI is causing a paradigm shift. Previous prediction methods function on a linear principle; cause and effect are clearly obvious. For example, a bank may deny a loan because the applicant is unemployed. However, many machine-learning algorithms, and especially neural networks, are black-box models that make precise, non-linear predictions. Only input and output are known, and even programmers have a hard time predicting the outcome. Therefore, even if they don't understand the reasoning behind it, users usually have little choice but to accept the algorithm's decision. However, developers are giving growing attention to unraveling the model's internal dynamics in order to return a profound, semantic line of reasoning tied to the decision.

Responsible businesses that utilize AI systems conduct extensive testing and place a huge importance on maximum transparency. They seek out opportunities for public auditing and reviewing, continuously conduct follow-up testing, disclose usage statistics and adjustments, and ideally make the source code public (open source). If the system works well, people will eventually realize that algorithms are better equipped to make decisions in certain situations and will consequently get used to accepting their decisions. Naturally, this only applies if the predictions are accurate.[157]

Decisions pertaining to controversial social issues are particularly delicate. AI's decisions are judged based on current social standards, so training language systems with old data can lead to problems. For example, AI trained to assist with personnel decisions may recognize that, in the past, management positions were primarily filled by men. It may then conclude that male applicants are to be preferred for these positions and hire accordingly.

One AI to solve several problems

Current AI technologies are highly specialized. The algorithm's problem-solving capacity does not extend to recognizing related problems — a connection that a human being would easily make. An algorithm trained to differentiate between dog breeds, for example, has no understanding whatsoever of the concept of a cat, and would be entirely incapable of discriminating a cat from a dog. So, in order to solve a similar problem, an entirely separate application must be created, or at least a separate dataset must be provided in order to train it. That is time-consuming, cost intensive, and leaves a lot of room for error, but it is also an unavoidable characteristic of specialized AI. Solving the problem is a step-by-step process, and we are only getting closer by decoding natural intelligence and further working on AGI.

How automation and AI affect the workplace

How will we work in the future? How will AI transform the work routine, the job itself, and the wage structure? Will there be sufficient jobs available, despite automation? Leading experts are divided. The majority of experts agree that our economy will benefit from automation, AI, and robotics. As a result, productivity is likely to increase, and while some jobs will be lost, new jobs will be created as well.

Jobs in unpredictable environments (landscaping, skilled trades, child and senior care, etc.) will be less likely to experience a significant amount of automation. This is largely because certain tasks are harder to automate, but also because automation is still less attractive for lower-wage sectors.

Open up for AI. It is not hype; it is a society changing mega trend. That means it is slower in the development than we think (caused by missing knowledge, standards, ethical essentials and investments), but the impact is way bigger than most of us can yet imagine. Read, meet, exchange and learn every day about one topic of AI – YouTube, TED and many conferences are good starting points.

Look at areas of your company that could be automated already, for example through RPA or Bots. Also have a look at the automation level and areas of your competitors (SimiliarTech.com) and initiate hackathons, workshops and intrapreneural competitions.

Train your kids and/or your staff in skills which a machine can't do, like art, design, empathy and philosophy. And take an active part in conversations that arise about ethics and responsibility, when AI is used.

SMART
SENSOR

immediate
data - transfer

Text: Daniel Heltzel, Monika Smith

A Status

Everything is connected

The next step is a huge leap: Millions, if not billions of new internet users are on the verge of going online. We're not talking about human beings, but rather machines. At first, the internet connected only people with each other, and now it's the teapot's turn. Or a large-size industrial robot. Or an intelligent lighting system. The fourth industrial revolution is bringing the Internet of Things to life with intelligent devices and sensors that collect data, make decisions, and report potential problems to human users.

The Internet of Things (IoT) sends and receives information ceaselessly, supporting the user in a task instead of requiring their attention. The Internet of Things is available in different versions. One is end-user focused, where human interactions with devices and objects are the main priority. In another, devices inform users when a specific event occurs, and can be controlled remotely. The industrial version (IIoT) focuses on manufacturing and industrial environments, as well as logistics, agriculture, and energy.

Intelligently connected industrial systems make manufacturing processes more flexible and increase efficiency. That makes a product development cycle shorter, saving money. Designs can be quickly and easily adapted, and smaller batches can be produced. Quick front-end processes are helpful in creating quotes and analyzing processes, which typically leads to additional innovations. Low-cost RFID chips make objects clearly identifiable. The broad availability of wireless communication and improved broadband networks are setting a solid foundation for the development of smart manufacturing (smart maintenance).

All this is based on sensors. The data they collect is used as a basis for automation and self-learning machines. This creates huge amounts of real-time data that needs to be processed in the shortest time possible. Big-data technologies and automation may therefore overlap in certain areas.[158]

Smarter sensors

The next step towards a comprehensive IoT is so-called smart sensors, wireless micro-sensors that not only collect data, but process it instantly. They can be widely used in physical environments as well as directly on people, and are particularly useful for national security and military applications.

The sensor market is expected to grow rapidly from $110 billion to more than $240 billion by 2022. Once sensors become more intertwined with the market for AI technology, they will seem indispensable.[159]

B Developments

Instant feedback, from anywhere

IoT and IIoT are about to change consumer behavior and modern manufacturing forever. By connecting software with hardware, they create a whole new ecosystem. Efficient individualization becomes affordable, which means customers and their product expectations are the priority. A digital cycle develops which has the ability to make the manufacturing process more efficient, recourse-friendly, and cost efficient.

Open API solutions — that is, programming interfaces that can be accessed by external users — are gaining in importance for businesses because they can link previously separate ecosystems. This allows third parties to develop applications for another company's products and offer services that they can then sell to consumers.

In the future, different aspects, from design to production and from delivery to customer feedback, will be linked. This can take place via software platforms that are designed to integrate the various applications and enable data exchange between separate sectors.

The future is decentralized

Industrial production generally follows a loop, from single-piece to volume production and back to single-piece production — all while avoiding production losses. The motto of the past was: The more identical products per production run, the lower the cost. This is a classic top-down approach: Production management has centralized control over all production processes.

In the factories of the future, the product itself will take the initiative. With its own internal chip, an unfinished piece finds its way across the production floor. It spots an unoccupied machine and utilizes it, and hey presto! It can be ready in time. This type of individualized manufacturing is a huge leap forward in terms of efficiency, down to the so-called batch size 1.[160] An industrially manufactured individual item might seem like a contradiction in terms, but it could revolutionize the factory floor.

Smaller businesses lack resources

Automation is unlikely to penetrate smaller shops anytime soon; the technical, operative, and economic barriers are too overwhelming. Many smaller businesses simply do not have the resources that would be necessary to invest in automated equipment or industrial robotics, or even train their employees accordingly.

Objects are getting smart

On our journey to creating an internet capable of connecting with the physical world and functioning without human interaction, we need "smart objects." Not only are they equipped with sensors to collect and categorize data, but they also make independent decisions based on that data. There is still no standardized identification of things and no uniform structure on which such a system could be founded. The question of how to supply it with power remains unanswered as well, as many objects are linked from a communication standpoint, but not yet from an energy supply standpoint.[161]

Standardized interfaces

The technology to link products, supply chains, and suppliers already exists. Nevertheless, most companies are far from implementing a completely integrated structure and are struggling with the process. The challenge is combining data from different sources – even different companies. In order to do this, the entire industry must agree on interfaces for the data transfer. Based on the example of the automobile or energy industry, you can see how elaborate that task is. "So far, combining electro mobility with renewable and decentralized energy production has not yet been successful."[162]

Standardization is a must in many areas, especially in data processing. The many different, incompatible communication protocols of wireless networks within the direct service area show how difficult it is to create uniform coverage standards. Without standardization, the diversity of protocols will certainly cause chaos in the IoT area. That is not cost efficient and not sustainable — in fact, it may even create the need for redevelopment.[163]

c Take–aways   <u>Smartware, IoT, and IIoT</u>

Visit CES and conferences like Blackhat and DefCon to stay on top of in the latest developments in regards to use cases, security, sensors and ideas, and exchange knowledge with other companies and groups with passion around connected devices.

Use IoT in your own environment. It can start by buying a connected lightbulb at IKEA to fully equipping your kitchen with IoT with self ordering fridges and intelligent cook processors. Get familiar with how the products and systems can interact and how you can benefit from them.

Even with an Arduino (https://www.arduino.cc) and some sensors anyone is able to develop simple solutions with a budget below USD 50, like a light controlling system, coffee maker remote control or simple security access management.

MY DIGITAL
OLD EGO

Text: Curt Simon Harlinghausen, Steffan Heuer, Christian Solmecke

Security

Text: Curt Simon Harlinghausen

No data is safe

When you leave your house, you lock your door. If you keep expensive valuables at home, you install an additional lock, or even buy a safe. And if you are a company owner and you have equipment worth millions sitting on your production floor, you hire a security service. In our analog lives, we understand how important security is. Unfortunately, in our digital lives, we tend to underestimate it – in business and privately.

A huge amount of data containing information about each one of us is already circulating around various networks and stored on remote servers. The more our devices link up with one another, the bigger the risk becomes that our data will be stolen or manipulated. Old passwords or social data can be used to remodel passwords, to create pretexts for human hacking or manipulate future stories. Digital existences can be literally wiped out in an instant. Whether we are referring to a PC, a self-driving car, a digital language assistant, or a military drone, any linked device can be manipulated.

The importance of securing our data cannot be overstated. Without the protection of our intellectual property, our whole society can be compromised: Our privacy and classified information are vulnerable, and preventing fraud and verifying the authenticity of information becomes more difficult.

The cybercrime threat has grown to "never-before-seen dimensions," according to last year's warning from Europol, the law enforcement agency of the European Union. In 2016, Germany's Federal Criminal Police Office (BKA) recorded more than 80,000 cybercrime cases, an 80 percent increase since the previous year.

There are countless different types of attacks: Malware, such as viruses or trojans; so-called DDoS attacks, which are meant to disable systems first; and "classic" hacking attacks, such as Metasploits and man-in-the-middle attacks. One type that has gained popularity among perpetrators is ransomware, software that encrypts data and only releases it after a ransom has been paid. One thing most of these attacks have in common is that their first target is not the computer, but rather the human being behind it.

People and their identities find themselves in the crosshairs. They are gate-keepers and the biggest safety risk all at once. Experts estimate that 95 percent of all cyber-attacks are caused by human error. Social engineering, also called human hacking, is a form of hacking that uses psychological methods and careful prepa-ration to manipulate victims to reveal information or allow it to be accessed. One example is the so-called tail-gating method, in which a person carrying a seemingly heavy box politely asks if you could hold the door to a secure building for them. Very few people actually question whether this person is even authorized to enter — and so the conman enters easily. It is becoming more common for businesses to hire so-called red teams, which uncover and document human security risks and offer training courses to raise awareness about social engineering methods.

Nevertheless, time and time again intruders are able to penetrate servers and systems with malware. Often they get in through human gates. However, even wi-thout human error, one thing should be remembered: The perfect software that of-fers 100 percent security does not exist. Because of high complexities, dependen-cies, and heterogeneous infrastructures, hackers, bots, and malware can usually find a hole in the system. Where there's a will, there's a way: Successful criminals have proven this time and time again. In 2017, the FBI was able to close in on nume-rous marketplaces across the darknet, even though the gate network was conside-red impossible to infiltrate securely and anonymously.

Intruders and guardians are in a permanent race with each other. At confe-rences such as BlackHat, DefCon, and Shmoo, you can clearly see the computer security industry's logic: If you want to secure a system, you must first try to hack it. Cybersecurity and hacking are really two sides of the same coin. Companies with data to protect need hackers to identify holes in their system. Microsoft, Google, and Facebook work closely together in this area using bug bounty programs. To-gether with developers, users, and hackers, they constantly discover security risks and work together to eliminate them.

Meanwhile, the other side never sleeps: Bots and crawlers (automatic search mechanisms and data collectors) are getting faster and smarter. With their help, many methods used to obtain information can be automated, and security gaps can be exploited efficiently. Often intruders are not smuggled in immediately in malware, but instead wait for certain events, or collect data in the background before exiting the system again.

The intruder's motivations can vary greatly. Carefully planned, large-scale attacks on companies or countries are often about industrial espionage or even influencing foreign governments or politics. The digital war between countries is getting more heated, even though it is kept quiet and discreet. Besides these well-organized criminal groups, there are also other hackers. For example, there are those who do not really have any malicious intensions but are simply driven by the challenge to outsmart the system — the hacker community calls them "script kiddies." They want to see how far they can get with pre-configured tools that are available online.

All these factors make encryption measures (cryptography), as well as decentralized verification technology such as Blockchain and hashgraphs, even more important for businesses. Modern cryptography deals with the security of confidential information, access protection, protection from manipulation, and data authenticity verification. It is all about identifying sources and securing the exchange of data and information. During this process, privacy laws must be respected and transparency should be made a priority for the audience. Verifying the authenticity of information is one of the biggest challenges that we will face in the future, in spite of all the technology and established verification methods that we already have in place.

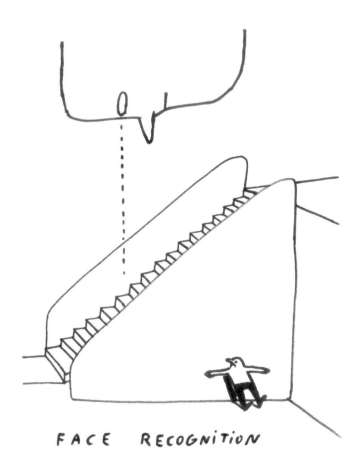

FACE RECOGNITION

TRANSPARENCY CREATES ACCESS TO DATA

Christian Solmecke on GDPR

A Status

On May 25, 2018, the General Data Protection Regulation (GDPR) of the European Union officially came into effect in Germany. At the same time, the German government passed a privacy act that partially modifies and concretizes the GDPR. The goal of the GDPR is primarily to create a uniform data protection law that is valid for all members of the European Union. Individual-related data must be better protected, while at the same time data traffic must be improved. In this respect, the GDPR represents a step in the right direction: It was absolutely necessary to unify the ragtag nature of data privacy laws.

B Developments

One priority of the GDPR is to strengthen consumer rights and provide users with more control over what data businesses have access to. Additionally, consumers now have the right to request information or even have data deleted. The GDPR also applies to companies that are not located in EU member countries, as long as they interact with EU citizens; this means that companies such as Google or Facebook also have to abide by the new regulations. This has already led to a number of changes: Not only have the two companies made sure that their data privacy statements and guidelines are compliant, but the way data collection is communicated is now much more user-friendly as well.

However, to smaller companies and freelancers, these rules are not practical and can barely be followed. In these situations, the new guidelines may feel excessive. The new rules stipulate that all data-protection processes must be recorded beforehand, along with the legal basis on which processing occurs. Especially for small businesses, this may prove quite cumbersome. The only hope is that eventually there will be a law that differentiates between certain criteria.

Fines for violations have increased considerably and can amount to 4 percent of a company's yearly worldwide sales. However, the main goal of these fines was initially to force large American companies to take data protection more seriously. One can only hope that the authorities will pursue any violations on the part of these companies. However, these tools may in fact primarily be used to go after smaller companies, since they are often overwhelmed by the conversion and unsettled by the media coverage of the GDPR. It will be absolutely crucial that, in the near future, specialized lawyers and data-protection officials train and support them in their processes. A large number of court cases are also to be expected in the near future, as fundamental legal questions must be addressed and the application of the GDPR must be fine-tuned.

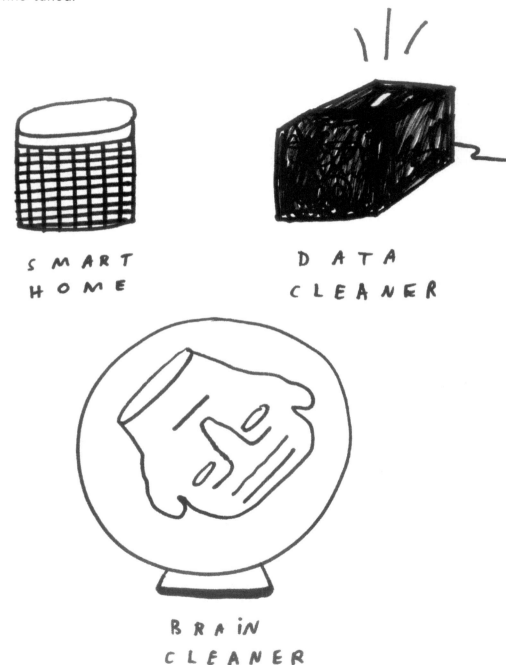

SMART HOME

DATA CLEANER

BRAIN CLEANER

Steffan Heuer on Privacy and Data Ethics

"It used to be said that data is the new oil. Personally, I think it's like nuclear fuel. It's becoming toxic."

Tim Berners-Lee, Inventor of the World Wide Web

A Status

When Silicon Valley's top dogs are publicly voicing remorse, the digital world must be in bad shape. Venture capitalists regret giving money to Facebook, while programmers are founding a Center for Humane Technology and talking about the destructive effects of the very apps and platforms that they helped to build. Tech managers are openly admitting in round-table discussions that they monitor their kids' internet access, or even forbid it entirely.

It's surprising that it's taken this long for the world-changing ideology of the California technocrats to start cracking, particularly from the inside. After two decades at the epicenter of the internet utopia, where everything is all about creating and sharing, many people are rejecting the utopian view of social media and making themselves less visible by withholding, disguising, or encrypting their data. Digital self-defense is hard work — it means not participating in social media when many of your friends and colleagues are, avoiding installing unnecessary apps, blocking trackers, and encrypting every single word you type. Convenience, network effects, and social and professional pressure try to convince you to change your mind and participate after all. This requires a lot of effort, and so far very few people are willing to make it.

However, since Edward Snowden revealed how fine the line is between commercial and government tracking, many things have happened to cause the digital climate to shift.

B Developments

This is a very telling time. The US is concerned about the damaging effects the internet could have on its civil society. Russian manipulation is only the tip of the iceberg; more and more people are starting to realize how their online and offline activities expose them to being stalked, manipulated, and used. Or, as Princeton IT specialist Arvid Narayan has stated, "The state of online privacy is society's problem and not the problem of an individual. We have a collective moral obligation to take action."

Now, new generations of internet companies are forming. Capitalizing on the weaknesses of the dominant platforms, they are committed to honesty and transparency. Even if Apple is only joining this movement for marketing purposes, it still encourages others to do the same. Founders are putting their necks out there for data ethics, i.e. handling data responsibly, and finding new angles to develop sustainable business models.

No question about it: The market is still dominated by the big guys, the rude guys. The ones who take before they ask, the ones who issue half-baked apologies or, worse, just ignore you when they get caught. You might say that they have to be callous, because apparently the future only belongs to those who set up large AI silos that can absorb data from hundreds of millions of users, then process it under unspecified principles and offer it to a few selective partners.

In order for start-ups that put data ethics first to have a real chance, users must get used to thinking before they post or host, and companies must be more conscious of which provider in which country they give their data or even parts of their value chain to. Newly founded companies such as Startpage, Cliqz, Wire, Clue, Protonmail, and Tesorit offer attractive products that are "made in Europe." These companies respect modern data-protection laws and set themselves apart from the large US platforms that have become prisoners of their own data-collection obsession.

If it is true that data is the most valuable resource of the near future, then founders and users have to be honest enough to admit that no resource can be harvested or refined without producing toxic waste products. We are already up to our ears in digital pollution.

The tech world is giving birth to a digital sustainability movement, and it is about time. Think tanks such as the Stiftung Neue Verantwortung (Foundation for New Responsibility) or the Internet Economy Foundation in Berlin represent promising developments in this direction. The leaders of this countermovement do not necessarily have to be totally abstinent or preach about radical "digital detox," nor do they have to be converts from the valley or lawmakers whose IT penny finally dropped.

We need a new generation of movers and shakers who are serious about data ethics for providers and digital self-defense for individuals. They are best suited to prepare us as a society and national economy for the age of algorithms.

We humans are the biggest security issue. Fact! Make a difference: If you have a Facebook account, download your copy of data and take a look at what they know from you (http://bit.ly/my_facebook_data).

Read websites like www.darkreading.com, www.defcon.org or even www. heise.de

Update your data security on a regular basis and make data security within your company a priority number one topic through continuous training, education and sensitisation. Have a top 10 security rule book for trust, passwords and handling of information (for example, a good password is at least 10 letters long, includes capital and lower case letters, numbers and at least one special character, AND excludes names, birthdates or well-known favourites).

Check if you comply with the GDPR regulations, call your legal advisor for a final bullet proof check.

BLOCKCHAIN :

INTERMEDIARY ARE PAST...

Text: **Jukka Hilmola, Marcus Prosch, Monika Smith**

A Status

Trust is good — Blockchain is better

Every system needs a central hub, a location where everything comes together. But what do we do if this center has a problem? Then the entire system goes down in flames. It's time to eliminate the center. Decentralized systems are on the verge of becoming reality.

Up until now, this was unheard of. Centralized systems (governments) run our countries and made the creation of empires possible. Take the Empire of China, for example. Its origins can be traced back to the first emperors that were able to unite countless local tribes and then form a centralized government. Likewise, with the great Roman Empire. Other systems, such as the financial sector, large companies, and social structures, are built the same way.

However, centralization is often vulnerable to corruption. It relies on intermediaries — go-betweens — who have everyone's trust. For example: Contracts are typically based on understanding and trust. In case of a breach of contract, a neutral party — such as a court — steps in to enforce the contract. Even financial transactions do not function without trust, such as the trust in the integrity of banks and central reserve banks. The system can be damaged by middlemen who abuse this trust and act against their orders.

Blockchain can solve this problem. It is a technology that publicly distributes data sets and allows permanent control through all involved parties with the aim of preventing manipulation. The development of a decentralized consent mechanism, which is the foundation of Bitcoin, offers an unprecedented chance to overhaul our reliance on traditional structures.

Many start-ups are using Blockchain technology to revive different industrial sectors. Currently, the usage of Blockchain is limited to individual projects that aren't linked to one another. The oldest Blockchain network and the most widely known is the digital currency Bitcoin, which saves transactions of payment units in blocks. Besides looking into other digital, non-governmental currencies, some countries such as Sweden, India, and Georgia are also experimenting with Blockchain technology. By evaluating Blockchain-based land register entries, they are trying to determine if it could be used as a system to manage public data.[164]

Everything is becoming decentralized

Blockchain provides security without trust. As such, it has the potential to disrupt not only the fintech industry, but also other sectors in which it is beneficial to save data in a way that secures it against manipulation. This actually includes every system that has up till now been run by central authorities: Ownership titles (managed by the state), contract details (managed by the courts), and payment processes (managed by banks). Go-betweens such as notaries, government agencies, and banks would be eliminated with Blockchain-based organizations. Instead, all relevant data would be public. This way, the parties involved are able to verify the data immediately.

In order to successfully make a global financial transaction, the buyer and the seller used to be required to utilize a trustee service to ensure all financial obligations were fulfilled. Third-party involvement generates additional cost. Besides that, worldwide fraud is feeding a market that is worth almost half a billion dollars annually.[165]

Manufacturers of luxury goods, the art and automobile industry, as well as other businesses that are easily affected by imitations or criminal activity are looking forward to a decentralized future. Start-ups are beginning to offer decentralized solutions in exactly these target industries, particularly to address corruption and fraud.

Developing countries are suffering under unacceptable discrimination in the current system, because many citizens do not have access to any kind of banking services. However, most typically own a smartphone, which means that they are connected and therefore not excluded from entering the new era of the global financial world — Blockchain technology, that is.

Alternative systems

Blockchain might be a popular buzzword at the moment, but it truly has the potential to become one of the most important engines of digitalization. It allows algorithms to complete transactions that are currently only available to people, and automizes the management of important data. This would clearly simplify and automate countless administrative and business processes.

In addition to Blockchain, other powerful alternatives are also forming. Take IOTA, a decentralized network for a democratic peer-to-peer economy which is based on tangle technology. Only the community participants can build consensus, and they are not rewarded for it, but simply do a part of the workload. Every transaction that a participant completes in the tangle network requires them to confirm two other transactions. This way, there is no unnecessary energy consumption, no transaction fees, and no dependency on the provider. Additionally, it enables micro-payment transactions, for example between devices, since classic Blockchain solutions often entail high transaction fees.

Not everyone is on board

Initially, people are often skeptical of a technology like Blockchain. The concept of centralization is deeply rooted in our minds, possibly even since ancient times, so it will be a while before the shift to decentralized thinking can be accepted. Furthermore, there are many market participants at risk of losing some of their profits to Blockchain, or worse, their entire business model might be in danger, because the decentralized technology makes certain services unnecessary or, at the very least, much more affordable.

In order to convince people to give Blockchain a chance, we need projects that show what it can do. Take the petro as an example: Venezuela, a country on the verge of bankruptcy, is attempting to redeem itself with its own cryptocurrency. The petro is backed by Venezuela's natural reserves of oil, gas, gold, and diamonds. If we can convince people to use Blockchain and give it a fair chance, then our economy and financial system will face a major overhaul.

The transformation to decentralization brings additional challenges for economy and society. Innovative companies all over the world have taken notice of the technology and are looking for ways to implement it. Integrating Blockchain into existing business models and company processes is not always easy. From a legal and social standpoint, the question also arises as to how to regulate this technology. We will need carefully designed general regulations that are capable of confining fraudulent systems without hindering innovation.

Energy guzzler Blockchain

Blockchain transactions are expensive. A decentralized system in which everyone is constantly checking on everyone requires exactly that: Permanent surveillance. This happens in Blockchain through so-called mining. Miners validate Blockchain contents and get rewarded with cryptocurrencies, usually either Bitcoin or Ethereum. This process is extremely computationally intensive and is therefore mainly carried out by huge Chinese server farms, at least in Bitcoin's case. It is, in theory, possible for individual miners to gain enough power to take over the whole of Blockchain.

However, more pressing is the problem that mining uses vast amounts of energy. More and more computing centers are moving to countries with lower energy costs, and are on the brink of causing an energy crisis in countries such as Iceland. The fact that computing processes are getting even more elaborate and therefore require even more energy is part of today's Blockchain technology. Some ideas on how to solve this have already been proposed: Vitalik Buterin, the founder of the cryptocurrency Ethereum, for example, is working on a less computationally intensive proof-of-stake method.

Another side effect of Blockchain is permanency. The implications of this are just now starting to become apparent. Once saved on the Blockchain, data will never again be forgotten. But what are we allowed to keep forever? Do we have a right to expunged data? We must debate these questions in order to find the right answers for our society.

IMAGINE
OF SOLID
MARKETS

c Take—aways   <u>Decentralization</u>

Learn to understand the basics of Blockchain and the idea behind decentralization. A good way to get a deep dive into this new technology is a workshop or an intense reading session of one of the Blockchain books.

What can Blockchain technology do for your company? Can you use smart contracts to bypass regulations and lower transaction costs?

Meet a Blockchain start-up and learn how decentralization could serve your company. Take a look at Provenance, a software company that uses Blockchain technology to build a traceability system for materials and products.

Get your head around Bitcoin, Initial Coin Offerings. Ether and newer coins/token.

Take a critical look at the recent ICOs. And also look at how other companies have developed, for example companies which did an ICO a year ago. On https://topicolist.com you can find a list of ICOs. Happy scrolling.

Commerce

Intro

Text: Monika Smith

It's been obsidian, silver, and gold, or galleons, cubits, and bitcoins. What we call it doesn't really matter — it's currency and it's what it represents that's important: value, trust, and power. Currencies today can empower us to shape our businesses into what we want them to be, create impact, manifest our purpose, and be part of the global affairs.

Traditional business models, including organizational structures, are changing. Modern companies are flexible and agile; their investment channels are brokered by agents who actually understand and support their ideas. It seems like a brave and bright new world. For larger, less adaptable companies, however, these developments could pose a threat.

Technological advancement offers businesses a remarkable opportunity to offer new products in new ways. In the online world, finding a product and completing a transaction can be done in a matter of seconds. But if you want to buy stocks, finance a house, or sell your company shares, payment processes still take time. Assets like gold, real estate, and fine art are even more difficult to transfer, requiring mountains of paperwork and lengthy procedures. Now, a change is happening. Digital tokens like cryptocurrencies represent physical assets, for example fiat money, making it possible to exchange in real time.

Step by step, our devices are removing the need for cards or cash, and as cryptocurrencies become more widely used, everyone will have a chance to participate in trading on the global level. Tailored to an individual's needs, delivered on time, and creating a valuable consumer experience from your wish list to your shopping cart to your house. This kind of human-centric targeting is based on data and happens on a daily basis to all of us — which brings us to one of the biggest challenges of our time: the quality and protection of data. So much is at stake as the global economies become ever-more inextricably linked. We know from 2008 what can happen when the system fails. Are we ready to deal with a new set of complex challenges on top of an already compromised system?

To help you design your business purpose in the field of commerce, this section includes chapters on Business Model Innovation, Token Economy, Payment Systems, Marketing, and E-Commerce.

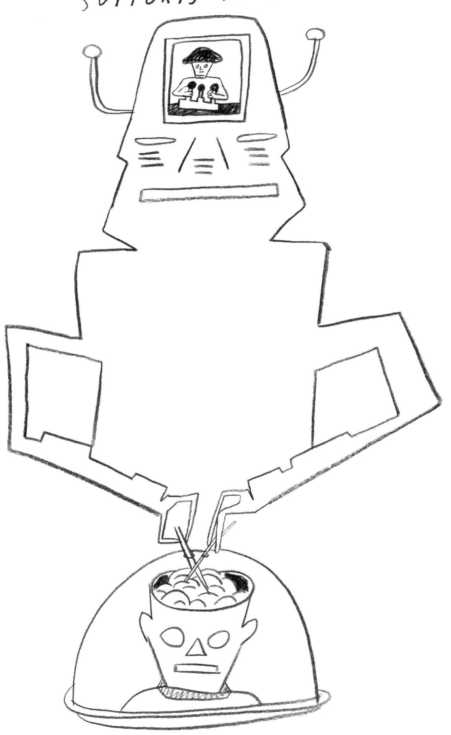

INNOVATION

BEATS
PROCESS OPTIMIZATION

Text: Don Spampinato, Scot Carlson

A Status

Supply-Chain optimization doesn't deliver like it used to

At the turn of the 20th century, Japanese businessman — and later founder of Toyota — Sakichi Toyoda invented an automatic power loom based on a new principle known as "jidoka" (automation).[166] Jidoka designed the machine to automatically stop running when a problem occurred. This intuitive manufacturing process ultimately became the foundation for streamlining Toyota's famous production system.

Toyota went on to design and roll out one of the most successful supply-chain optimization processes ever. This concept is still used today as part of applying lean production to enable businesses to improve quality, reduce waste, increase productivity, and save money; and this, in turn, allows them to price their products to benefit both the customer and the company.

Eventually, nearly all companies adopted similar processes.[167] However, instead of the anticipated success, they started to notice a downward trend: while competitive advantage, savings, and ultimately sales growth did increase, their profit margins mysteriously shrank.

Process optimization outmaneuvered by innovation (pivoting business models)

Example: Amazon

In 1995, Jeff Bezos launched a website with the intention of creating a business that would scale exponentially, develop one of the most streamlined operations ever, and generate billions of dollars. A bold ambition: Bezos was up against some of the most successful and well-established companies in America. After learning that e-commerce was projected to grow by 2,300 percent,[168] Bezos made a list of products that could be efficiently marketed online, including computer hardware and software, CDs, videos, and books. Bezos picked books. He converted his garage in Bellevue, Washington, into a distribution center, and partnered with wholesale companies for access to the most popular books at the time. With this lean business methodology, Amazon was able to aggressively undercut the competition due to the absence of storefront costs, and, thanks to the internet, a far greater reach than any mail-order catalogue could have achieved.

What appears now to be a very straightforward set-up for your everyday online company was revolutionary in 1995 — and has resulted in an ever-growing platform driven by lean business processes.

The utilization of both lean supply-chain optimization and lean business processes design is the driving force behind Amazon's ability to position themselves more competitively.

B Developments

Design thinking reaches maturity

Amazon is resolutely focused on its consumers' needs. Its products are high quality, low-priced, and able to be ordered and received with a speed none of Amazon's competitors have been able to rival. These three value propositions are driven by consumer interest. In fact, Amazon has been known to "obsess over customers, not competitors."[169] Today, there is much to be said for the merits of customer-centric strategies over product- or service-led innovation. A recent report from the Design Management Institute revealed that, in the last ten years, design-thinking-led companies "have maintained significant stock market advantage, outperforming the S&P by an extraordinary 211 percent."[170] The key takeaway? It appears that those organizations that are quick to adapt their operating models to ever-changing consumer demands will maintain a competitive advantage over those that remain stuck in their ways.

Transparency reigns, and it pays to be "human"

There is a saying: a brand used to be a black box, and marketing could paint whatever picture it wanted on the surface.[171] Today, that no longer holds. Thanks to the internet and its plethora of information, companies and their dealings have never been more exposed. The "black box" is now clear: almost all of its activities and inner workings have been made transparent. A person's consumption of certain brands or products is now taken as a sign of their values, which is why it is increasingly common for individuals to broadcast their social awareness through the brands and services they choose to support — or reject. Unsurprisingly, the "brands rated by consumers as the most intuitive and understanding comprise a diverse mix of industries, business models, and personalities. What they all have in common is an ability to translate key customer imperatives into action, demonstrating the relationship behaviors that drive loyalty, advocacy, and growth."[172]

The emergence of holacracy: not as "flat" or unstructured as you might think

Distributed "hybrid" leadership models, while not new, are gaining traction. Many companies want to act like a start-up, so it's no wonder that they're beginning to ask themselves whether their traditional, hierarchical organizational model is outdated or holding them back. While this is far too broad a topic to be fully explored here, it is worth noting that companies seeking to explore different models often mistake a "flat" organizational structure for a holacratic one. The two terms are not equivalent: Holacracy is different from a "flat" organization in that it "envisions a scenario where accountability and leadership are equally distributed among the workforce."[173] Holacracy seeks to redistribute responsibility by eliminating unnecessary managerial layers, but it does still provide a solid, clear structure.[174] A "flat" organization, on the other hand, often suffers from a lack of structure due to unintentional ambiguity and — sometimes — "land-grabbing" activities, all of which can lead to operational inefficiency and lack of collaboration.

How can we design human-centric organizations?

Traditional supply chains were about reducing costs as much as possible in order to provide the consumer with the most affordable product on the market. In recent years, however, there seems to have been a change: Consumers are no longer necessarily looking for the cheapest product. Instead, they want what they deem to be the best option for themselves. Recent trends indicate that consumers are now looking for the most convenient – but also the most socially responsible – ways to acquire what they need. The fastest and easiest way to procure something is no longer necessarily the cheapest, or, say, the most ethically produced and/or environmentally friendliest. The most successful organizations of the future will therefore be those that can adapt to the ever-changing needs of their audiences and adjust their procurement, pricing, and distribution strategies – as well as their organizational structures – accordingly. Behaving ethically, knowing and designing for the consumer, and continuously investing in "organizational R&D" will provide the benefits previously achieved through more traditional means like cost-cutting, process improvements, and supply chain optimization.

Convenience and consumer experience first – products and services will follow. Identify your value propositions for your company, product or service, challenge those with different perspectives and try to explore small (MVP, PoC, One-Product-Shop, etc.), "incubator" projects which experiment with new ways of working or new consumer experiences.

Check out Alexander Osterwalder's Business Model Canvas to try out a systematic approach to business model innovation. Osterwalder is the co-founder of Strategyzer, and you can find some great material on their website https://strategyzer.com/. On http://masterfacilitator.com/canvas-collection you can find a list of over 50 canvases for all kinds of topics. Get inspired: make use of this incredible selection of resources and start innovating.

"Done is better than perfect," says Mark Zuckerberg. You can do it: prototype, test early, learn what went well and what didn't, think about how you could do better, and iterate. Then do it again. This will not only save you a lot of time, but it will also make your business model future-ready and keep your organization engaged.

Commerce

Text: Shermin Voshmgir

Token economy—the future of currencies?

There is a widespread misconception that Bitcoin and tokens that have derived from similar technologies are currencies comparable to fiat currencies like EUR, USD, etc. In fact, Bitcoin and other crypto tokens are not currencies in the traditional sense, but rather:

• A new asset class

Bitcoin and other native Blockchain tokens that have derived from it have more resemblance with commodity currencies of the past than with state-of-the-art fiat currencies.

• An operating system for a new type of economy that transcends the geographical boundaries of nation states. The protocol of the Bitcoin Blockchain coordinates people who do not know or trust each other across national boundaries of without the need for classic, centralized institutions or legal agreements.

While it might be counterproductive to call Bitcoin a currency, as it sparks a lot of controversy and is not entirely true, Bitcoin does have similarities with money as we know it. The biggest challenge that we face when trying to explain or discuss Bitcoin, Blockchain, and other crypto economic technologies, is that we are trying to explain new phenomena with old terminology that sometimes doesn't do justice to the full range of possibilities that these new technologies have to offer. In order to understand the full range, we need to dive into the following questions: What are the roles and functions of money? What are Bitcoin or so-called tokens anyway? Can a token economy eradicate the monopoly of nation-states on issuing money?

Functions of money

Skip this if you already know what money is.

The primary purpose of money is to facilitate an economic exchange of goods and services within and between economies. It makes economic exchange much more efficient than gift economies or barter economies by avoiding the inefficiencies of such systems, like the coincidence of wants problem. Here is a list of money's most important functions:

• Medium of exchange

Money is an efficient technology for mediating the exchange of goods and services, because it provides a tool to compare values of dissimilar objects.

• Measure of value

As a unit of account, it's a standard numerical monetary unit of measurement of the market value of goods, services, and other transactions. It is (a) a basis for quoting and bargaining prices; (b) necessary for efficient accounting systems; and (c) a prerequisite for the formulation of commercial agreements that involve debt.

• Store of value

Money must have the ability to be reliably saved, stored, and retrieved—and be predictably usable as a medium of exchange when it is retrieved. Its value must remain stable over time, since high volatility is counterproductive for trade, and inflation reduces the value of money and diminishes its ability to function as a store of value.

• Unit in which debt is denominated

If money has the status of legal tender, it is a unit in which debts are denominated, and an accepted way to settle a debt. When debts are denominated in money, the real value of debts may change due to inflation and deflation.

Properties of money

To fulfill its various functions, money must have certain properties:

• Liquidity

Easily tradable, low transaction costs, no or low spread of buy and sell price.

• Fungibility

Units of money must be capable of mutual substitution. Every token (physical or virtual) must be treated equally, even if it has been used for illegal purposes by previous owners.

- Durability

Ability to withstand repeated use (not vanish, decay, or rot).

- Portability

Assets must be easily carried and transported.

- Cognizability

Value must be easily identified.

- Stability

Value should not fluctuate too much.

Types of money

Different types of money have evolved over time. In modern economies, the dominant types of money are so-called fiat currencies.

- Commodity money

is an object which has an intrinsic and standardized value in a local economy. The value derives from the commodity of which it is made of: gold, silver, other rare metal coins, salt, barley, animal pelts, cocoa, or cigarettes, to name just a few examples. The price is determined by a metric of perceived value in conjunction to one another in various commodity valuations or price systems economies.

• Representative money

Money is a medium of exchange that represents something of value, but has little or no value on its own. It's a claim on a commodity: like gold or silver certificates, or paper money and coins backed by gold reserves.

• Fiat money

Unlike a commodity, fiat money does not have an intrinsic physical value. Its face value, which is denominated on the banknote, is greater than the value of its material substance.

Fiat money

Fiat money is established by government regulation, similar to any check or note of debt. It derives its value by being declared by a government to be legal tender, which means that it must be accepted as a form of payment within the borders of the country for all debts, public and private.

The assigned value results from the fact that governments can use their power to enforce the value of a fiat currency. In modern economies, most money in circulation is not in the form of bills and coins, but rather entries in the digital ledgers of a bank, which manage money saved in current accounts, checking accounts, and other financial instruments.

The money supply of a country consists of currency (banknotes and coins) and, depending on the particular definition used, one or more types of bank money (the balances held in checking, savings, and other types of bank accounts). Bank money, which consists only of records (mostly computerized in modern banking), forms by far the largest part of broad money in developed countries.

Fiat currencies have evolved over time. While banknotes and coins used to be pegged to scarce commodities like gold and other precious metals in the past—as representative money—gold backing has drastically declined during the 20th century. Most currencies today are barely pegged to commodities. Central banks influence the money supply with monetary policy—which means that they print more or less money as they see fit. But how is does all this relate to Bitcoin? And what is Bitcoin anyway?

Trends Bitcoin: a crypto-economic operating system

While Bitcoin was originally designed with the purpose of creating P2P (person to person) money without traditional banks, the underlying Blockchain technology that makes it happen has proven to be a gateway to a new type of economy (crypto economy), and a new type of distributed governance (crypto governance). Please note that the terms crypto economy and crypto governance are new, not yet fully defined, highly controversial, and somewhat complementary or overlapping. For now, let's stick to analyzing the functionalities of Bitcoin:

- Public and permissionless payment network (P2P network)

Bitcoin is a P2P payment network between a geographically disparate group of stakeholders who do not know or trust each other, which does not require centralized institutions like banks, credit card companies, PayPal, MoneyGram, and the like. It is permissionless, which means that anyone can become part of the distributed network, either by creating a Bitcoin wallet (Bitcoin account number) and starting to send and receive Bitcoin, or by becoming a Bitcoin miner by downloading the protocol and verifying transactions, thus potentially mining Bitcoin, which equals earning money.

- Bookkeeping Tool (asset management)

Furthermore, Bitcoin is a distributed bookkeeping tool that keeps track of who owns what, including all transactions ever made, in a public and transparent way. The role of cryptography is to guarantee transparency while maintaining the privacy of individuals. This distributed ledger is a new form of transferring value in a public and transparent way, circumventing the need for data silos.

- Crypto-economic governance tool (governance layer)

The P2P network of stakeholders, as well as all assets, are governed by the rules defined in the protocol of the Bitcoin Blockchain. Monetary policy is also pre-defined in the protocol. Transactions are automatically enforced if and when the majority of the network agrees that a transaction is true. The crypto-economic mechanism design incentivizes all stakeholders in the network to verify transactions according to pre-defined rules by performing computational work—proof of work—that allows them to mine Bitcoin, i.e., to create new Bitcoin. This mechanism design can be altered in a protocol update, in the form of a soft fork or hard fork. The crypto-economic incentive mechanisms, including the monetary policy of Bitcoin, can be altered by majority consensus among network participants. The conditions of such software upgrades are partly defined in the protocol and partly unclear.

- Bitcoin is mined to keep the network safe (security function)

Some people who don't fully grasp how the Bitcoin Blockchain works claim that Bitcoin has no function or value. This is not true. Bitcoin is, in fact, the output of a productive function, governed by crypto-economic incentive mechanisms, that makes sure that a distributed network of actors who do not know or trust each other validate transactions according to the pre-defined rules, in an attack- and collusion-resistant and fault-tolerant way. The act of mining bitcoin keeps the network safe!

- Bitcoin needed to pay for transactions (commodity/utility)

In order to send a transaction from Bitcoin Wallet A to Bitcoin Wallet B, you need to pay transaction fees in the form of Bitcoin tokens, which will be rewarded to the miner who mined the block where your transactions were included. This means that the token has a utility function within the Bitcoin network. Bitcoin is the native commodity of the Bitcoin network.

Why Bitcoin is not comparable to fiat

- If anything, Bitcoin is commodity money, not fiat money

While Bitcoin has certain properties of money, it is more comparable to commodity money than to fiat money. As long as people use the Bitcoin network for services that need to be paid in the native commodity (Bitcoin token), the token has a value in itself, as it is used to pay Bitcoin transactions. The commodity aspect of so-called cryptocurrencies becomes more evident in Bitcoin derivatives like Ethereum (where you need to pay for computation in ETH) or the Sia Network (where you pay for storage with an SIA), since those networks were not designed for P2P remittance (like Bitcoin), but P2P computation (Ethereum) and P2P file sharing (Sia).

- Decentralized production, price determined by supply and demand

The nature of commodities is distributed control, much like Bitcoin. No single government or other entity controls the mining of gold, silver, oil, etc. Production is distributed, and the prices of those commodities are determined by supply and demand on commodity markets, much like the price of so-called cryptographic tokens are determined by the supply and demand on crypto exchanges like Kraken, Bitfinex, Ploniex, Coinbase, and the like. As opposed to fiat currencies, no single centralized entity, like a government or central bank, can influence the price of Bitcoin or other crypto tokens.

- Higher liquidity than classic commodities

As opposed to classic commodities that are traded on classic exchanges, cryptographic tokens (Bitcoin, Ether, and the like) have higher liquidity, due to the nature of Blockchain-based P2P remittance. Exchange and remittance are easier, faster, and cheaper, and, if you don't use third-party services like banks or stock brokers, entirely P2P.

- Price fluctuates

Bitcoin is not regulated by a centralized institution, but determined by supply and demand in markets, and is currently highly volatile. Because the fiat currencies of most modern economies have fluctuating exchange rates that are determined on Forex markets, national institutions can perform currency intervention — such as foreign exchange market intervention or currency manipulation — as monetary policy operations. Governments or central banks can buy and sell currency in exchange for their own currency to manipulate the market price. Why? Governments usually prefer stable exchange rates, as excessive short-term volatility erodes market confidence, generating extra costs and reducing companies' profits, which keeps investors from investing in foreign financial assets. Therefore, the biggest difference between cryptocurrencies/-assets and fiat currencies is price volatility. With hedging and stablecoins, etc., on the rise, price fluctuations might be a non-issue in the near future.

- P2P payment network

In addition to having many similarities with money, the underlying payment network allows you to circumvent classic banks, credit card companies, PayPal, Money Gram, and the like. Bitcoin is money without banks or bank managers. The role of the bank in money remittance is substituted by the smart contract of the Bitcoin network.

- No centralized institution governs Bitcoin

The Bitcoin token is the currency of the "distributed internet tribe" called Bitcoin. Monetary policy and all other governance rulesets are determined by the protocol of the Bitcoin Blockchain. Code can only be upgraded by majority consensus of network actors; the details of this process are too complex to go into here. While the original vision outlined in the Bitcoin white paper was more decentralized, reality has proven that network actors can in fact collude to gain more control (e.g., Bitcoin mining pools versus individual miners).

Token economy—the future is here

To sum up: Bitcoin is a new asset class, and has pioneered an operating system for a new type of economy in which it has become feasible for everyone to issue their own purpose-oriented token, either by forking the Bitcoin protocol and creating their own purpose-oriented native Blockchain token, or, even more simply, by creating an application token on top of the Ethereum Blockchain with a few lines of code. With this new technology, it is now possible to create completely new types of economies, where we can model behavioral economics into a smart contract with the purpose of incentivizing certain behavior—like planting trees instead of cutting them down by mining "tree tokens" (aka making money) when trees are planted. People can also be incentivized to reduce their CO_2 output (traveling by bike instead of by car, or using solar power instead of fossil-fuel energy) by mining "Co_2 tokens" (i.e., making money) when they reduce their CO_2 emissions.

Cryptographic tokens allow us to create a digital representation of physical assets—so-called asset-backed tokens—with the result that these assets can now be traded at much lower transaction costs. Some of these assets might then have higher liquidity than on current markets (commodities like gold, gasoline, etc., but also real estate, and many assets that have been less liquid in the past).

The future is already here, but most people are not aware of it yet. As of January 2018, around 1,400 cryptocurrencies (all with different properties and purposes) were listed on coinmarketcap.com (Cryptocurrency Market Capitalizations). However, we are still at the very beginning of this revolution. There are a few challenges ahead of us:

Price fluctuation of crypto assets
Sustainable mechanism design for purpose-oriented app tokens
General education about the potential and also threats of the token economy
Unclear and Balkanized legislation
Definition of money as we know it

Outlook

Recently, Venezuela and Kodak have both announced their own cryptocurrencies. If 2017 was the year of ICOs (initial coin offerings), 2018 will be the year of tokenization. Things are changing and they are changing fast. Only time will tell how this will affect the role of money as we know it.

c Take-aways   Token Economy

Get involved and experience it first hand. Make a small, for example €200, investment in one or two cryptocurrencies (for example IOTA or Ether). Be part of it and learn about the process, the challenges and technologies on the fly. At the same time get in touch with Blockchain Hubs around the world to educate yourself about Blockchains, smart contracts, tokens, ICOs and the Web3.

Evaluate if your company is ready for the tokenized world, and try to set up one token project (at least as on a conceptual level) to make sure you understand that world. It is useful to hire an expert to facilitate the first steps or hold a hackathon.

Collect 12 questions through researching the internet and discussing with colleagues and try to answer every month one question from a corporate perspective, at least as a high level view.

REALISATION OF MICRO PAYMENT

Text: Nimrod Lehavi, Monika Smith

A Status

Transitioning from money- to data-based markets

For a long time, strict regulation meant that the financial sector was largely sheltered from the upheavals of digitalization. It was often possible for financial companies to ignore digitalization completely and simply carry on as usual – all without losing their position in the market. But this is changing rapidly. Like their counterparts in other industries, financial service providers are struggling to remain competitive. In the past, banks served as information channels for markets, but they are losing this role in the new, data-rich markets, which have access to significantly more diverse and valid sources of information. Banks thus risk losing an important source of income, and are on the lookout for ways to adapt.

They've experienced increasing competition from fintech (financial technology) companies. These usually have the advantage of more modern data technology and more effective information processing; when assessing credit default risks, for example, fintech companies take a person's education and employment into account, which also helps people who do not yet have a sufficient credit history to obtain a loan. Since many fintech companies exist primarily virtually, their lack of physical infrastructure allows them to operate much more cost effectively than traditional banks — a price advantage they pass along to their customers, along with improved service and higher security standards. As a result, large financial institutions are transforming into IT companies, making a point of acquiring the smaller fintech start-ups driving innovation in the payments industry.

New payment methods

We pay for things dozens of times a day, but the way we do it is changing. Digitalization, intense competition, and more transparent consumer preferences are all affecting how we approach financial transfers. It is essential that businesses understand and meet their customers' changing needs if they wish to remain relevant.

International payments are to this day slow, expensive, and opaque. One reason for this is that they still have to go through the 600-year-old system of corres-pondent banks.

Although at the moment cash and cards still dominate the payment-transacti-on landscape, mobile payments are increasing. These new technologies are especi-ally popular with young people, as well as for certain types of transactions, such as sending money to friends. Today's digital payment industry is dominated by compa-nies like PayPal, Venmo, Square, and Stripe. These services allow for payments bet-ween people (P2P), between people and businesses (P2B), and even between bu-sinesses (B2B). Payments are made via app between individuals at the time of sale. Mobile payments offer many advantages: They are user-friendly, customer-oriented — and in high demand. By 2019, the total amount of mobile payments is expected to exceed $1 trillion. A service orientation and streamlined operations are absolutely key: The easier it is to pay and get paid, the better.

B Developments

Payments anytime, anywhere

Soon, all it will take to make or accept a payment — anytime, anywhere — will be a tap on a smartphone. Ensuring that a company can cooperate with these new payment systems is crucial to improving its customers' experience. In the future, we expect to see payment-service providers and financial institutions changing the way they operate or joining forces with new players to offer and support an ex-panded payment ecosystem. Banks will form new fintech alliances to work directly with organizations, such as the American TD Bank and the fintech company Moven, which have collaborated to provide TD customers with access to Moven's money management app.

Blockchain as an agent of progress

Hailed as the way of the future, Blockchain has become the hottest buzzword in the financial industry. Financial institutions are busy testing out ways to use and implement cryptocurrencies and the Blockchain technology that supports them for their systems and transfers. Cryptocurrencies and Blockchain-based systems will be at the forefront of the new financial landscape due to their many advantages: They make large transactions easier, faster, cheaper, and more secure. Since Block-chain processes are decentralized and transparent, every transaction can be easily

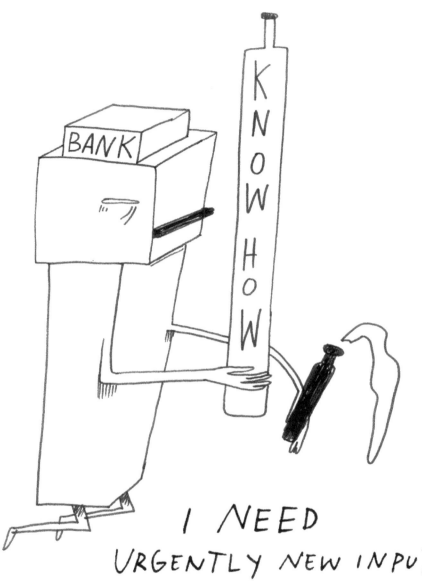

I NEED URGENTLY NEW INPUT TO TRANSFORM MYSELF.

tracked, thus making fraud extremely difficult.

There is still a significant gap, however, between what is possible and what is common. Most shops and supermarkets do not accept payment in cryptocurrencies, though this will almost certainly change once a critical mass of users has been reached. In the near future, simpler Blockchain systems for cryptocurrencies will exist that are suited to trading on mass markets. Even people who have never had a bank account before will have an online account with a high level of service and customer proximity.

Digitizing payment systems

The innovation bottleneck that used to dominate the traditional financial sector has broken open, and the industry is now changing and re-inventing itself all the more quickly. As it does, our basic understanding of banking, financial services, and investment advisory is changing, too. In future, we will no longer need to physically visit our bank (there may in fact be no physical bank to visit!). A credit card account will be nothing more or less than software code; our banks, in a sense, will be everywhere and nowhere. This will naturally have an influence on the customer experience, as well as on regulations and security measures. The transition to digitized and decentralized payment processes raises questions about the role that other technologies such as Blockchain, augmented reality (AR), the Internet of Things (IoT), and biometrics will play in our financial transactions. Any and all of these may affect both how consumers experience the payment process and how governments regulate the industry.

All this puts great pressure on banks and governments alike. New orientations — as well as new possible restrictions — are on the horizon. Modern banks must strive for flexibility: They must not only offer their customers the services they want and expect, but also build upon and expand new relationships of trust. From artificial intelligence and IoT to chat bots and voice-controlled banking, banks will aim to inspire confidence. The days in which a potential customer would be impressed by a stately stone building with a prestigious address are over. Customers today are critical and informed: A bank that offers intelligent discount systems and a focus on customer satisfaction will enjoy a competitive advantage, while one that assumes its customers are too comfortable (or too lazy) to switch financial service providers will suffer in these times of simple and comprehensive data portability.

Adapting to new circumstances requires considerable investment in infrastructure and a shift in the internal culture. But in the end, it's all about creating value for the consumer, who will be attracted to the organization that makes their daily life the easiest.

If you haven't already done so, try out one of the new services like N26 or Revolut or sign up for a payment system like PayPal, Google Pay, Apple Pay or Amazon Pay. Simply open an account, download their app and do banking via app. Also check out AliPay and the Tencent Finance ecosystem around WeChat.

Review the way your customers pay and want to pay often. Offer them the latest payment methods. Paying should be convenient, simple and with added values.

Talk to start-up founders from fintech companies. Usually they are happy to share their insights and bring you an idea of possible impacts and use for your own company, as well as open discussion with members of generation X, Y or Z about money, payment and their vision of the future of finance and payments.

HIGH FLEXIBILITY

Text: Curt Simon Harlinghausen, Pascal Fantou

A Status

The five major marketing drivers of today

Five major developments are currently driving marketing: digitization, content marketing, marketing automation, big and actionable data, and personalization on scale. Digitalization means that more and more advertising takes place online and in apps (particularly as the reach of TV declines), leading to the continual growth of the out-of-home market. Content marketing is the new social media, and since display advertising is becoming increasingly ineffective, new formats are needed to reach and activate target groups. Marketing automation is one big development: Increasingly programmatic advertising is accepted by publishers, agencies, and advertisers alike, its measurability and automatic selection mechanisms promises better efficiency for all. Data — whether big, smart, or real-time — is already the oil of the digital economy and the gasoline for the engine of digital transformation when it drives (better) decisions and measures. Even amid digitalization, however, personalization plays a major role. Contextual in timing, amount and format, in real time or with the right emotion set matching the realtime behavior, individual and contextual marketing campaigns can activate positive emotions and address intentions to encourage purchase and customer loyalty. Those five drivers are an essential part of a complete and cleansing transformation of a whole industry – the impact is bigger than we expect, but also it is a continuous process, and fast.

Channels

The number of channels is growing, but those that actually determine a market remains fairly constant. Classic channels like TV and radio are losing range and relevance; Google and Facebook are now the great gatekeepers of traffic and media channels. Other strong players, such as Amazon, are moving to enter the digital market as well. In addition, the prevalence of mobile devices presents both brands and media with challenges in terms of format, tracking, and interaction.

Creativity vs. execution

"Creativity makes the difference" was long the credo of an entire industry. Today, however, it's more often the execution of a creative idea that makes the difference. A mediocre idea executed boldly can attract more attention than an ingenious idea executed indifferently. Why is this? The answer lies both in developments within marketing itself, as well as the increased importance of digital communication.

While creativity may seem like a fundamentally human endeavor, automation may soon play as significant a role in marketing as it does in other business processes. Machines and algorithms cannot yet come up with creative campaigns or ideas themselves, but things may be different in the future. With the help of AI (machine learning) and digital empathy, it is only a matter of time before systems will be able to develop individual measures, campaigns, and ideas on their own.

People are becoming media

Influencer marketing is gaining traction as brands look for better and more effective ways to reach their target groups. By advertising sponsored products online, popular social media stars themselves are turning into a form of media — and charging accordingly. Just how sustainable this development will ultimately be, however, is anyone's guess.

Lead nurturing: contextual communication in real time along the entire sales funnel

Lead nurturing becomes ever more relevant for its ability to reduce the distance between company and customer; co-creation is just one example. Greater proximity to the customer represents both an opportunity and a challenge: The customer expects to be treated as an individual whose history is known each time they come into contact with the company. The art is to manage this subjectively perceived closeness in a scalable way without sacrificing the company's own authenticity, while minimizing the competitive space.

Lead nurturing is surprisingly uncommon: Only one-third of all companies practice it. The remaining two-thirds of companies underestimate the importance of lead nurturing, perhaps assuming that their CRM efforts are adequately covered by simply sending out newsletters on a regular basis. But lead nurturing is, at its heart, a user-oriented concept, and this is an idea too important to be dismissed.

Moreover, companies all too often neglect processes of forming hypotheses, testing, implementing, and continuously improving in the midst of the day-to-day operational frenzy. In such circumstances, lead nurturing cannot possibly achieve its potential. The fact is, no one buys a car their first time at the dealer. Decision-making periods are growing shorter, but that does not negate the need for a more holistic view (including competition) of the journey.

B Developments

The number of possibilities, varieties, and subgroups of marketing have exploded in recent years. Each type offers different advantages and disadvantages, depending on the situation and the specialists involved. The trends and challenges we can currently observe in marketing reflect this growing diversity.

Content is king, real-time content is King Kong, and content with context is Donkey Kong

Content was crowned king some time ago, and it's only growing more powerful as its reign continues. The reason for the monarch's success? The value of communication and marketing is no longer in empty advertising messages or brand promises, but in the content it provides (photos, videos, editorials, podcasts, reports, etc.). Thus, more and more brands are trying to expand to become content media. In the future, content will be tailored to the individual phases of the marketing funnel, adapted to the target groups, dynamically generated and compiled, delivered, measured, optimized, and personalized in real time with contextual information.

The future of marketing is in increasingly automated technology

Technology is the biggest driver of change in marketing and, like water, it's unstoppable. Technical solutions (DMPs, retargeting, etc.) and automation have already become key parts of most stages of business operation, from creation, implementation, measurement, CRM, atomic design, asset orchestration, cross platform synchronization, service, nurturing, A/B testing, and surveys to personalization and individualization.

REAL TIME is KING KONG!

The future of relevance and context

From ads and content to social media, relevance has become a significant concern as the pressure to produce effective advertisement and reduce costs increases. To stay relevant in a rapidly changing environment, a company requires in-depth knowledge of two things: their target groups, including behaviors, needs, and motivations, ideally in real time and in context; and the activities of their competitors, in order to be able to select and deliver specific messages, content, and formats. Relevance and context are both questions of data: Moving forward, both will rely more and more on sensors, smartphones, and the networking and aggregation of information sources in order to function precisely and in real time. As recent news has shown us, however, this is not without its risks: Even hugely successful media companies are vulnerable to manipulation and influence.

Focusing on the consumer – the real new purpose of communication (marketing)

"Consumer centricity" has been a buzzword since 2016, and is often used in connection with digital transformation. In order to put consumers at the center of attention, however, we need a broad and in-depth understanding of their behavior, as well as of touchpoints and their connections to the communication and sales funnel. Only those companies that develop user journeys, enrich them with data, and understand the difference between need and intention can create customer-focused models. The future of these journeys will be shaped by predictive analytics and journey data models.

Traffic is an underappreciated component of marketing

Traffic — both on- and offline — is a largely underappreciated piece of the marketing puzzle. The quality of online traffic is just as decisive to an internet company's success as casual customers, attracted on the street by an appealing window display, are to retail. A company should therefore attempt to maximize its traffic in both physical and cyberspace. With online traffic, for example, it is important to select targeted sources and providers that can easily record and analyze traffic history. Qualitative online traffic is poised to play a much greater role in marketing plans of the future through data enrichment — and because it's one way to crowd out the competition.

THE DECISION
FOLLOWS YOUR
EMOTIONS
AND NOT JUST
LOGIC.

Automated performance marketing

As traditional media and marketing strategies continue to lose their effectiveness and appeal, companies are looking for new ways to measure their marketing success. Performance marketing (SEO, SEA, CPC, or CPL-based marketing) is all about measurability, and a growing proportion of marketing budgets is already being invested into it. If the desire for consistently measurable indicators persists, automated performance marketing will be just around the corner.

E-commerce as media platform

More than merely a sales channel or advertising surface, e-commerce is now gaining importance as a media platform. It is not for nothing that Amazon offers a greater volume of media with each passing year: In the USA, online providers and e-commerce platforms already dominate TV advertising. In Germany, specialized accelerators like ProSiebenSat.1 (P7S1) have sprung up in recent years to invest heavily in e-commerce start-ups. As e-commerce continues to grow, it will only become more relevant to marketing, which will be able to make use of its new formats and possibilities.

Messenger marketing along the Chinese model

No single Western company can compare to China's WeChat: as both a messaging and social media platform and a mobile banking and payment service, WeChat is a "super app" boasting over 1 billion active users. Messenger marketing in the rest of the world is likely to follow WeChat's example, and has the potential to become a significant new marketing channel. The biggest advantage: Users can decide for themselves which brands to follow, either actively or passively. Technologies such as bots and AI mean that the "on-demand society" will be able to access information, products, and services instantly and at any time. In a future of new technologies and developments, messengers will become hubs of both payment and communication.

Accessing consumers in times of stricter data protection

Touchpoints are more relevant than ever, and not only when it comes to journey models and outsourcing media campaigns. Ever since the introduction of attribution models and touchpoint benchmarking, every single touchpoint has had its own role. As new data protection regulations make it increasingly difficult to collect personal data, a knowledge of consumer access points will become more and more important. Understanding a consumer's behavior at a touchpoint will provide valuable insight into phenomena like lookalike audiences and behavioral twins.

Moving away from the watering-can principle

The watering-can principle refers to treating all elements in a given context equally, without considering that their individual needs may differ: Giving all plants in a garden the same amount of water, for instance, whether they're cactuses or cattails, or applying the same marketing principles to all target groups irrespective of age, location, or media habits. In order to maximize relevance and media efficiency, it is important to let go of the watering-can principle and to think instead about specifics. Platforms such as Google and Facebook, with their vast knowledge of their users and their behavior, have exacerbated market segmentation. As a result, target-group marketing has become an essential skill. The problem, however, is that creating content for a specific target group is significantly more difficult and time-consuming than simply compiling a selection of target groups. The parameters and possibilities for addressing target groups will, however, continue to increase. Even one-to-one marketing will become possible, although it may not make sense for all brands, products, or services.

High-quality tracking

Anything that can be made measurable should be — and preferably in as automatic, networked, and real-time a fashion as possible. In fact, the market is not far from achieving this — were it not for legal hurdles like data protection. Tracking your own websites or apps using cookies, pixels, or digital footprints is just as standard as the use of heat maps, eye tracking, and social media monitoring. Data use and protection is still a complex and contested field. One great task of the future will be to find a responsible and effective solution to data management and bring a sense of order to data systems, sources, and providers. The quality of data – following the 3Cs principle: Complete, Consistent, and Correct — will also become increasingly important.

Content is king, Context is kinkong – understand consumer behavior in the context of timing, touch points, competitor activities and content engagement. Develop your own context model and editorial plans in relation to segments and their motivations.

Create end-to-end consumer journeys of your eco-system with different layers (touch points, intensity, data sources, emotions, etc) and perspectives (consumer, company, prospect, etc) and develop a tracking solution to ensure you follow the complete journey, for example as a funnel or reoccurring model.

Read Amy Webb's yearly report on Tech Trends where she presents the most relevant and recent technology trends in a very crisp and hands-on format. Experience her passion for what she does. See her talk at SXSW in Austin or watch her on YouTube. www.futuretodayinstitute.com

Learn to understand and handle data and treat it with care and sophistication. Get your KPIs right. Take your time to ensure a proper KPI set up which leads to measures and continuous outcomes (Dashboard). Data-driven campaigns, performance marketing, and smart data nurturing all require clearly defined and specific KPIs, as do social media monitoring (for crisis prevention, for example) or attribution models (for more effective marketing budget distribution). This will make a tremendous difference. Think about the possibility that in the future, KPIs will be divided into values for people (simple) and values for machines (complex).

Text: Martin Sinner

A Status

The limits of growth

Not so long ago, before Google solidified its monopoly, even larger online shops could still count on getting additional traffic from various channels at a relatively low cost. Many shops even intentionally focused on a single traffic channel, while others were more or less neglected. Only a few players truly engaged in professional online marketing across all meaningful channels. In e-commerce, these efforts were primarily geared toward SEM/SEO with PLA (product listing ads), participation in marketplaces such as Amazon and eBay, and affiliate marketing. However, large players in particular eventually reached the limits of growth and were forced to expand their organization in order to capitalize on all relevant channels. This expansion presented a number of challenges: Larger teams made operations more complex, while attribution and evaluation of the various challenges became more difficult.

Evaluating purchased traffic more precisely

Attribution technologies and logic have become indispensable to online marketing. Evaluating traffic quickly and correctly is crucial in the face of increasing demands on traffic efficiency. Currently, many online marketers in e-commerce are working to improve the quality of purchased traffic by using existing customer data. To do this, they need access to data that used to be largely unavailable.

Modular shop systems and surrounding ecosystems

The increasing complexity of e-commerce is leading to numerous changes in tech stacks: Many shops or their service providers can no longer handle most of the technical implementation themselves. A number of solutions have arisen to rectify this, among other things, a complete ecosystem for shop systems that offers a wide variety of possibilities for improving the conversion of a shop, from recommendation engines to CRM tools and exit layers. As shop systems become increasingly modular, we are also moving towards an exciting world of microsystems, which will affect even large suppliers of shop systems.

Consolidation of small shops with low revenue

To avoid the hassle of managing their own shop, some retailers mainly sell their products via Amazon and/or other marketplaces. Amazon's advertising system offers unknown brands the opportunity to appear in the better sales tiers. Many retailers have been able to take advantage of this to position their brands very well, especially on Amazon, even if the brand otherwise lacks visibility. Compared to other countries, the landscape of German shops is still quite extensive. In other countries — particularly the USA — the number of retailers in terms of audience is already considerably lower. An astonishing number of shops in Germany still have an annual revenue of less than 1 million euros. Many of these shops run exclusively on free SEO traffic; Google, however, is constantly trying to turn free traffic into paid traffic, and will likely force most of these players to either close down or consolidate.

The forest for the trees: attention to detail at the expense of platform orientation

Globalization aside, when it comes to e-commerce, the German market differs considerably from the American one. In terms of concentration, consolidation, and online/offline market shares, Germany lags behind Great Britain and the USA. Germany's comparatively slow internet service, on both mobile and desktop devices, is certainly one factor in this. At the same time, there are many more providers per inhabitant in Germany and thus also many small shops, even if Germany trails behind the US in marketplace models. German companies are clearly struggling to adapt to the platform economy. Regardless of the platform economy, however, it can only survive as a monopoly in the niche — or even as its own platform (such as Zalando). Amazon is not yet as dominant in Germany as in North America, though it's likely to become so. German e-commerce has pioneered other areas, most notably in the reliability of click-and-collect, although that's more of a sideshow. Click-and-collect is a good example of the fact that German market participants often can't see the forest for the trees.

Slow growth and multichannel concepts

Although growth is likely to prove difficult in the coming years, there are still opportunities in the mobile sector. Especially in Germany, the About You model could certainly be applied to other areas such as home accessories, gifts, lifestyle, or designer fashion.

Multichannel concepts represent another interesting prospect, though more for manufacturers than retailers. One current example is Bianchistore.de: The Italian road bike manufacturer Bianchi was able to develop its multichannel strategy in the German market with the help of a local retailer. The cooperation was so successful that Bianchi has announced it will be expanding the model internationally. Thus, particularly in new markets, Bianchi is transforming from a manufacturer marketing via retailers to a retailer and manufacturer marketing itself — without cannibalizing its existing local retailers. A manufacturer's transformation into a retailer can work to the retail network's advantage, as long as local retailers are able to sufficiently distinguish themselves in their service. But this also represents a challenge for retail, since manufacturers are now gaining increasing market shares.

c Take–aways   <u>E-Commerce</u>

If you are a small e-shop owner, make sure you use modular systems instead of trying to build your own. Shopify (www.shopify.com) is one option to take a closer a look at.

Don't be late for Christmas. As obvious as it might sound, be early for all relevant seasons. Make sure your products and services are available and up-to-date, and your staff is prepared.

Check-out processes are the last barrier for successful sales. Check your own purchase journey – test, optimise and especially collect user feedback (live testing, eye- and mouse-tracking, surveys, etc) across your complete customer segmentation to understand what can be more convenient, how the newest technology can simplify the check-out and what makes you better in comparison to your competitors.

Planet

Intro

Text: Monika Smith

If you look long enough into the night sky, you might even see us — spinning through space, one small speck of light, a green-blue planet in an unimaginably vast universe. Sure, there's other planets and stars, black holes, and all sorts of unexplainable matter around, but there's nothing like us.

It begs the question — why do we act as if our planet and all its natural wonders are inexhaustible? We are smart, with all of our convenient technologies, and yet we are completely stupid. It is clear that we need to implement a radical shift in every aspect of our world. The problem is, it all seems way too complex to do anything about — plus, we're so used to the way things are. We're caught up in a profit-driven economy, where growth seems to be the only chance of survival.

There is movement, and hope. A new generation of entrepreneurs is establishing companies that make a profit — but not at any cost. In the energy sector, many countries are attempting to transition to clean energy, developing intelligent digital processes to make greener solutions more cost effective. And sustainability has become a recognized management topic, reaching into the production and supply chains of large corporations. Those are valuable attempts, but we are not there yet.

It is not at all clear whether constant growth helps us progress or makes us happier. Perhaps now is the time to create a new standard to measure the state of a society, apart from gross domestic product. The question is: Will it be enough, or is it too little, too late?

To help you design your business purpose as regards the planet, this section includes chapters on Sustainable Entrepreneurship, Energy and Resources, Production and Supply Chain, Growth Economy, and well-Being and Happiness.

WHERE TO GOES THE TRIP?

AT THE END
NOT JUST
SKIMING.

SUSTAINABLE
ENTREPRENEUR
SHIP

Text: Philip Siefer, Alexander Langer

A Status

How entrepreneurs can save the world

It was not so long ago that divisions were clearly marked: Economic success and career versus doing "good." Suit or Birkenstocks; Porsche or bicycle; growth or sustainability: A new generation of young entrepreneurs is rejecting this either/or approach — they want to achieve both. Social entrepreneurs create companies that generate profits while simultaneously trying to improve the world.

Social entrepreneurship is a new trend in corporate management. It uses traditional supply chains to generate incomes and then converts them into charitable structures. This idea is becoming more and more popular: In 2015, there were already about 70,000 social enterprises in Germany.

The predecessors of social enterprises are non-governmental organizations and traditional charities. Their general goal is to improve the world by investing in social action for a more inclusive society, assisting the disadvantaged groups that aren't involved in the return of capitalism. People are motivated to work for such institutions for altruistic reasons — they want to do the right thing.

So-called effective altruism has very recently become a new focal point for business culture. It is driven by people who bring in entrepreneurial spirit and economic expertise — they want to do good, but in an efficient way that aligns with the company's objectives. The benefits of a charitable donation are quantified and donations distributed based on a set of predefined key figures. Whereas traditional charities rely on emotions to prompt generosity, effective altruism uses statistical analysis to determine where a donation will do the most good.

The concept of social entrepreneurship involves using all the levers of capitalism and the market. The big difference: The products and services are fair, sustainable, and generated by the concept of pull rather than push. This represents a significant paradigm shift for companies and consumers. Classical charities depend on donations, and thus on the goodwill of the donors. Social enterprises, on the other hand, are part of the normal process of product or service creation. Because the customers do not donate money, and instead consume services or products, they participate in acts of goodwill and take comfort in feeling that the company they're supporting has concerns beyond the mere maximization of profit.

Moving towards positive change

As the sustainable entrepreneurship movement becomes more widespread, it has taken on various forms, such as ecopreneurship, focused on ecology-driven innovations; start-ups founded by NGOs; or the fundamental restructuring of existing companies towards sustainability.

Sustainability is increasingly becoming an essential part of profit-oriented business models. Stefan Schaltegger, professor of sustainability management and head of the Center for Sustainability Management (CSM) at Leuphana University, Lüneburg, sees sustainable entrepreneurship as a driving force of this development: "Sustainability has become a recognized management theme throughout the economy and has become a movement that is not only influenced by a few pioneers, but by broad changes. Entrepreneurial success is increasingly linked to how well sustainability is incorporated into corporate DNA. It now involves audits of environmental management systems or the employment of large CSR departments towards the sustainability transformation of the business model; including an explicit consideration of the entire business environment."[175]

Performance instead of execution/completion (relationship via to-dos)

This transformation has ramifications for the future of work. Working in a sustainable company gives many people more than just employment — they feel fulfilled. As jobs increasingly become outsourced to artificial intelligence and robots, jobs with a sustainable purpose will help attract the best talent.

Employers will have to adapt to this. The values of the current world of work are strongly influenced by industrialization: Productivity is the central measure of work. By these standards, artificial intelligence (AI) inevitably beats out human workers. Machines and robots are much better than we are at precision work, and they don't need to take a break. That's why companies will increasingly hire people with skills that are less easy to reproduce, such as creativity or innovation design.

Get out of the niche

Scalability is still the biggest challenge for the industry right now. However much we see some businesses take up this approach, on a global scale, social entrepreneurship is still a niche phenomenon, and it is not yet seen as a real alternative to normal business. Added to this is the question of whether small-scale changes go far enough. Having a sustainable label is not necessarily a guarantee that businesses are really effective in applying sustainable outcomes to their products or services.

Despite some good projects, we have yet to see a really big success story. There are no big players in social entrepreneurship comparable to Snapchat or Facebook in the digital industries. Social entrepreneurs are still considered by many to be nerds who sacrifice themselves and live esoterically. For many social entrepreneurs, this perception of sustainable business as exotic or novel is a fundamental problem. It downplays the issue of sustainability, when in fact, in an environment of finite resources, it should be the foundation of all economic activities. It could be argued that social entrepreneurship should be the norm, and that forms of enterprise that primarily serve to maximize profit margins and stock values should be the exception.

Public perception is thus critical for social entrepreneurship. It should not be considered as a nice but ultimately insignificant idealistic project; otherwise the idea won't take hold. The industry needs to attract both highly qualified talent and customers in order to become an appreciable economic power and generate a real impact.

Climate change is real

There are still far too many people who deny climate change and claim that they do not believe in scientific evidence. Convincing these people — to whom, regrettably, even the president of the United States seems to belong — is proving to be a difficult task. Regardless of the sceptics, companies have a responsibility to move ahead. Our entire future is at stake: Will we manage to live here permanently, or is the late Stephen Hawking right, and we will soon have to plan our departure from "our very delicate planet"?

Think about ways your business can offset its carbon footprint or use and implement sustainable methods. Have a look at the 17 Global Goals for Sustainable Development (https://www.globalgoals.org/) in 2030. These goals were set to end poverty, fight inequality and stop climate change. Any small step is better than none. Create a workshop day at your company to investigate on how your company can contribute towards reaching those goals.

Work on your sustainability strategy. Does your company's purpose foster a sustainable business development? Which consumption patterns are initiated? Which lifestyle does it support? Get support in doing so. There are many interesting new consulting firms that can help you prepare for the future and make a positive impact on the world.

Take a moment on a clear night to look out at the moon and the stars. Think about the universe, about how vast it is. And about us, being part of it.

ego vs. eco

ICH HABE BURNOUT.

Autoren: Friederike Rohde, Monika Smith

A Status

The transition has not yet been made

The direction Germany intends to take is clear: "We must achieve decarbonization this century — that is, the complete transition to carbon-free economies." The German chancellor, Angela Merkel, announced at the Petersburg Climate Dialogue in 2015 that Germany would aim to cover its entire electricity consumption by renewable energies by 2050. But there is still a long way to go. Such a supply is not at all possible without a smart power grid, which will be defined later.[176]

Overall, energy consumption in Germany is not declining. The long-term trend shows that only heat consumption is declining, while fuel consumption is almost constant and power consumption is increasing.[177] Digitalization is a contributing factor: Processors and monitors are becoming more power-intensive, and more data centers are being built.

As technologies advance, new devices have to be manufactured, thereby requiring even more energy and raw materials. Due to short innovation cycles, the average service life of electronic devices is relatively brief.[178] As a result, the demand for rare earths is increasing, and the amount of electronic waste is piling up. The fact that the individual devices themselves may become more efficient and thus more economical unfortunately does not compensate for this. For example, even though the environmental impact of a single smartphone is comparatively low, the seven billion smartphones sold in recent years have already consumed 38,000 tons of cobalt, 107,000 tons of copper, and 157,000 tons of aluminum.[179]

This phenomenon even applies to renewable energies: Steel is used in wind turbines, and photovoltaic cells contain rare metals. Here, too, the question of resource sustainability is still highly relevant.

All sectors must be involved in a genuine energy transition. Private households account for more than a quarter of German electricity consumption. The rest is shared by industry (28.2 percent), transport (29.5 percent), as well as trade, commerce, and services (16.2 percent). Industry and trade are always better placed to plan their energy needs and therefore adjust their consumption. In the transport sector, however, about 98 percent of final energy consumption is fuel, and only about 2 percent is electricity.[180] As it stands, we're still a long way from any credible energy transition — even with the federal government's ambitious goals. The Earth Overshoot Day, calculated by the Global Footprint Network organization, shows where we might be heading if we don't use our resources more sustainably: It marks the date on which humankind consumed as many resources as the planet can reproduce within a year. In 2017, that was the case on August 2. If the whole world consumed as much as Germany, this limit would have been reached on April 24.[181]

B Developments

Digital solutions for smart distribution

Renewable energies require a different approach to the gathering and storing of energy. Power is created locally and fluctuates, as solar and wind sources change over the course of a day. The number of producers is increasing because electricity is no longer generated by a few larger power plants, but by many wind turbines and photovoltaic systems, and distributed over an increasing number of small operators[182] As such, the distribution and control of this complex energy system is particularly important.

That's where smart digital solutions play a vital role. Smart technology and big data, fueled by innovative business models, need to work together to optimize energy across different sectors.[183] A digitally networked energy system in which energy flows are measured, controlled, and traded in real time allows for a much more efficient system. When power is short at one site, surplus power can be drawn from another.

This vision has been discussed for more than fifteen years using the concept of smart grids (smart energy networks).[184] Now, there is a technology that could finally make the dream of the energy market of the future come true: Blockchain. Using this denominational database technology, citizens could act as so-called prosumers (producers and consumers) of energy in real time.

There have already been some initial attempts to do this. Democratic systems based on peer-to-peer solutions, such as the decentralized non-profit platform Energy Web Foundation[185] or the green energy trading platform WePower Network,[186] are revolutionizing the existing system. Other pilot projects, such as the SINTEG project C / Sells, rely on a kind of subsidiary energy system. The idea: Energy should be generated, stored, and consumed as much as possible at the local level. Such a network consists of many small-scale energy cells which generate their own supply.[187] This would considerably reduce the need for energy transmission and the system could operate with fewer high-voltage routes.[188]

Smart meters, the next generation of energy meters, provide energy usage information directly to suppliers and allow the end user greater understanding of their energy usage. The EU aims to replace at least 80 percent of meters by 2020.

Networking makes you vulnerable

As the energy system becomes increasingly connected, it becomes more vulnerable to outside intrusions. Cyber-attacks are a direct threat to the stability of the system and the security of the energy supply. For experienced hackers, accessing entire smart home systems or logging into photovoltaic controls is relatively easy. Resource scarcity, extreme weather events, and natural hazards also threaten the stability of the energy system. This makes comprehensive data protection and IT security for the energy sector an urgent topic.

Even today, the energy system is characterized by a high level of redundancy; that is, there is more infrastructure than is necessary for the actual operation of the system. This redundancy is generally an advantage, and we must expand and reinforce it in order to be able to withstand future threats. System-specific software is being diversified, cyber-defense centers are being set up, and decentralized units have been created so that individual parts of the system can function independently, even if others fail.[189] For some experts, open source (software) is an important component of a future digital infrastructure, since closed, proprietary systems make the user dependent on the respective provider, instead of allowing for collaborative development.

New digital hopes and the issue of resources

Blockchain is generally seen as a revolutionary force in the energy sector, mainly because it allows secure transactions between two parties, independently of a higher authority.[190] This transparency could make energy suppliers and intermediaries superfluous. Although the technology is not yet mature enough to handle millions of transactions in real time,[191] initial evidence indicates its great potential for the future. For example, in a pilot project in Brooklyn, New York, citizens can use a platform called Smart Contracts to trade their PV electricity directly and automatically within their neighborhood.

Ironically, current Blockchain technologies consume so much energy that, at first, they seem to stand in the way of an energy transition — after all, the goal is to reduce overall energy consumption. The Bitcoin Blockchain, for instance, currently consumes approximately 29.52 terawatt hours, as shown in the current Bitcoin Energy Consumption Index.[192] Bitcoin consumes more electricity every year than the entire country of Ireland. However, some Blockchain developers, such as Vitalik Buterin, the inventor of Ethereum, are working on lower-energy variants. It also remains unclear how Blockchain technology should and will be regulated.[193]

But it's not only Blockchain. Digital systems are all faced with the same dilemma: Although they are supposed to reduce energy consumption overall and revolutionize the energy market, they themselves require energy. Significantly, the energy requirements for telecommunications networks and data centers will increase from 18 TWh in 2015 to 25 TWh by 2025.[194] This amounts to 20 percent of all available electricity in the world. (https://data-economy.com/data-centres-world-will-consume-1-5-earths-power-2025/)

Energy transition and poverty

Energy transition and its accompanying effects impact every single one of us, as individuals, companies, and nation-states. As a result, a number of societal issues are bound to crop up. For example, privacy protection can't be easily reconciled with the desire to digitally connect as many households as possible.[195] Equal access is also an issue: What if only privileged homeowners can benefit from the advantages of being a prosumer, actively engaged in the energy market? And, rather than helping to reduce energy poverty, what if smarter technologies allowed energy companies to act much more quickly based on instantaneous data collection, and simply turn the power off?[196]

Such questions are rarely touched upon in the discussion of the opportunities and risks of digitalizing the energy system, but acknowledging these and other important questions is vital. Even if new digital technologies are indispensable for a sustainable energy system, it is also clear that technology alone will not solve our ecological and social problems.

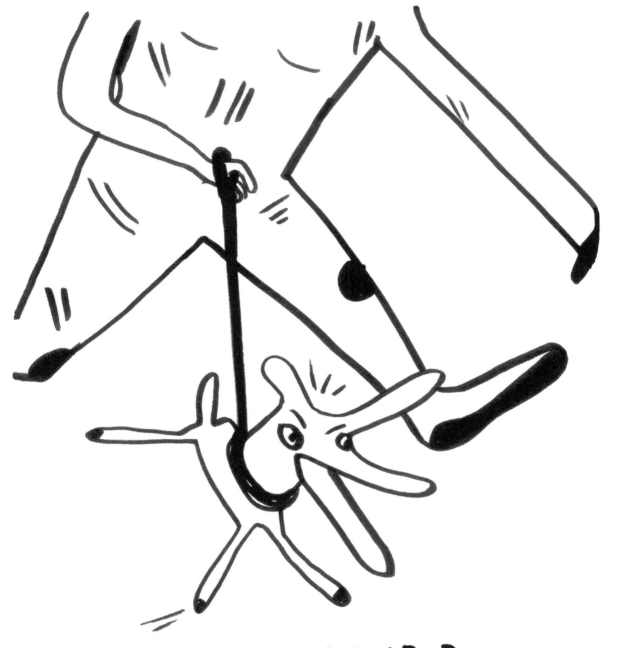

HOW CAN I ESCAPE?

GETTING INDEPENDENT FROM LEADING SUPPLIER?

Switching off the light during Earth Hour isn't enough. Commit to being a real part of the energy revolution, and improve your whole company's energy consumption. Communicating this approach in your PR and advertising helps to spread the word.

Follow the same principle at home. Try consumer-centric energy systems that control your energy consumption only if you need it. Pay attention to which products you buy. How much energy do they consume, and how long do they last?

Share your experience and knowledge with your colleagues and teams. Get some energy experts including start-ups in to share their experience. Then hold a contest about improving energy consumption in your company and its environment. Make this contest accessible to the whole company and share the results afterwards.

THE PILE OF RUBBISH GROWS.

Text: Maren Beverung, Monika Smith, Katharina Zwielich,

A Status

A growing mountain of garbage

We produce too much garbage. We know this only too well, but that doesn't mean that anything is being done about it. How much is too much? Two point one billion tons per year, to be exact — almost eight times the weight of all people on earth combined.[197]

And it mostly comes down to the way we produce goods. Practically all of the products we buy have a long production path behind them before they reach us, the consumer. Something as banal as a pair of trousers is an incredibly elaborate product, from the source of the raw material to the point of sale in the store: There is the cotton production, which consumes a lot of water in countries that often have little of it, and the dyes for which highly toxic chemicals are used, which in most cases are then emptied into the nearby river. People work extremely long hours for very low wages and then have to deal with major health problems. In the end, the trousers will probably not be worn for long, since fashion changes quickly, and the quality of production is often poor.

The end consumer is not the biggest waste producer — on the contrary: Most of the waste is generated along the supply chains. According to the United Nations Food and Agriculture Organization (FAO), one-third of food produced is lost or wasted, an equivalent of 1.3 billion tons per year. In the Global South, about 40 percent of this loss is due to harvest (referred to as "post-harvest loss") and processing. In developed countries, the same percent occurs on retail and consumer levels.

Although all this is well-documented,[198] environmental and social improvement is progressing at a painfully sluggish rate.[199] To make matter worse, our resources are finite. In short, we consume and waste faster than we regenerate and recycle.

Auditing for responsibility

There are certainly some creative approaches to tackling these problems. Social and environmental audits are a common tool through which companies can communicate their standards, at least to first-tier suppliers, and to which they can refer if misconduct is publicly documented by a supplier.[200] However, it is not possible to guarantee sustainable production solely through auditing. The underlying problems are too complex, and are furthermore stymied by wide-scale deception and corruption in the auditing business.[201]

In the end, most companies prefer to produce where it's cheapest, since consumers love cheap products and prioritize low cost over longevity.[202] Despite all efforts for sustainability and recycling, the balance of global production is correspondingly disastrous: The proportion of fully recyclable products, just like the entire chain of socially responsible manufactured products, is close to zero.[203]

B Developments

From the supply chain to the circular (closed-loop) economy

As the mountains of trash grow, our finite resources start to dry up, and labor exploitation gains increasing press coverage, consumers are beginning to demand more accountability. For this reason, cleantech innovations and new production designs are being developed.

Ecological trend: the circular economy

The waste generated from making a product tends to become a resource for a new product, which eventually becomes waste, which in turn becomes a resource, and so on. Such cycles already exist in natural ecosystems, and they constitute the model of what we now know call a circular economy. An increasing number of companies and start-ups are ambitiously attempting to implement a waste-free economy that completely dispenses with hazardous and environmentally harmful materials.

The Ellen McArthur Foundation defines a circular economy as a system where products and services are traded in closed circles or "loops." In this so-called cradle-to-cradle approach, the products or materials are preserved for the maximum amount of time. That means that all material inputs and outputs are seen as nutrients, either technical or biological. Technical nutrients can be recycled or reused with no loss of quality, while biological nutrients can be composted. A circular economy design requires systemic thinking that considers all the factors and consequences of the entire production in order to develop a resilient, scalable system.

In the textile industry, there are some attempts to put such systems into practice. The Swedish company Nudie Jeans produces jeans made from sustainable cotton. In repair shops, old Nudie jeans are mended. Customers can return their jeans and have them recycled — this is, at least in part, a circular economy. The British brand Ananas Anam has gone a step further: Founder Dr. Carmen Hijosa has developed Piñatex, a leather alternative from the waste products of pineapple production. In place of waste, income is now being generated, and at the same time a sustainable alternative to leather products — which have a large ecological footprint — is created. The example shows that more can be done than merely minimizing the negative impact of a product — a cradle-to-cradle design can create real added value.

Social trend: Supply chains are becoming networks

From the raw material to the end customer, each product passes through many stations, often distributed over the entire globe. At each of these points in the supply chain are people, and only when these people talk to each other do the production processes stand a chance of being improved. Instead of stringing together anonymous production stages, the supply chain can be considered as a unifying element between people.

For example, what happens if a European buyer comes into direct contact with workers in Bangladesh? They may develop a greater understanding of each other and of their respective needs. Actual contact and interaction makes the work more tangible and allows people to participate in decisions that directly affect them. A network that connects representatives of the entire production process across all levels can better handle the challenges at each stage of production and establish responsibility. This relationship, working across the entire supply chain, enables sustainable collaboration.

A first step in this direction is manufacturing transparency. Some clothing manufacturers provide tracking numbers so that customers can see where the cotton was produced. This is equally useful for suppliers who are involved in manufacturing the product, in that they can make sure they are joining a supplier network that shares their values.

Although the first steps towards the circular economy and networks have already been taken, there is still a long way to go. The United Nations has recognized the need for new production designs. The Sustainable Development Agenda of 2015, a collection of global sustainable development goals for the year 2030, also addresses sustainable consumption and production conditions. The goal is "doing more and better with less": It's about creating valuable jobs and increasing quality of life, reducing environmental and social costs, and fighting poverty. This requires a systematic approach and cooperation between the various parties within the supply chain, from the producer to the final consumer.

Sustainability as part of the business model

How does our waste become a resource again? And how can we establish authentic relationships between all partners in the supply chain? This requires a holistic approach.

Many large companies are trying to tackle the negative effects of their production methods through new agreements and certifications. It is tempting for companies to "greenwash," laying claim to sustainability but actually doing little to limit their environmental impact. For the most part, certifications such as carbon-offset programs don't go far enough. What's needed is a fundamental change from within, by implementing sustainability as a central part of the business model.

Sustainability begins at the design stage. Designers need to create products that minimize waste, in accordance with the circular economy design.

Challenges are plentiful: Often, suitable, value-preserving recycling methods are unavailable; the high cost of research projects is another obstacle.

The success of a circular economy model also requires a change in consumer perception and behavior. Sustainable products require more time to develop, due to research and design modifications. Consumers will have to accept higher prices for the products they buy. The numerous subsidies and grants for cleantech start-ups from the public sector are critical to helping sustainable companies get off the ground.

The new model is circularity, where waste is a new raw material. Reduce waste and separate your trash. Make it re-usable and make it easy for your employees and team members to do the same by offering clearly labeled trash bins. This should become an important part of the company culture.

Go to the factory floor and bring your team along. Initiate regular contact between your local team, your suppliers, and the manufacturers. Talk to the people who really produce, who do the hard work. Meet them in their working environment. It is often hard to understand the needs of workers who do not live the way we do.

For some inspiration, have a look at case studies and the latest trends in circular economy projects. Gunter Pauli gives a hundred inspiring examples of circular economy innovations in his book Blue Economy.

How do your products travel? Air, truck, ferry, or are they produced locally? Review your supply chain efforts, and if possible, reduce travel and use eco-friendly means of transport.

GROWTH AS A LOOP?

PARDON ME?

Text: Monika Smith

A Status

Relentless growth at all costs

It sounds like a very attractive proposition: more income, technology that makes our lives easier, less work; in short: a good life. In the 1930s, the British economist John Maynard Keynes predicted in his paper "Economic Opportunities for our Grandchildren" that in one hundred years, people would only have to work for only three hours in order to live a good life. Freed from economic constraints, people would finally have time for things like charity work and art. We are rapidly approaching 2030, and unfortunately, it turns out Keynes was wrong. Although today's economies are richer than ever before, people are not working less.

The reason is simple: We are constantly striving for more. In order for a country (or business) to be considered healthy, it must grow a certain percent — that is, at least, the defining thought of modernity.[204] In many economies, the goal of steady growth is above many other – if not all other – goals. More of everything; or, as economists would say: economic growth.

The quest for growth conflicts with the fact that we inhabit a planet with limited resources and share it with a growing world population. This is not news: Already in 1972, Meadows et al., in their study The Limits to Growth, used various computer simulations to show that exponential growth will inevitably exceed the limits of our natural resources and the resilience of our ecosystems.[205]

Slaves to the system?

Most economists see the need for change. However, such a change does not just depend on corporate will. Consumers also play a major role in the success of sustainable business models. In Germany, for example, household consumption accounts for a quarter of all CO_2 emissions. The production of consumer goods is not even included in this calculation.[206]

Consumers influence the entire supply (value-added) chain with their purchasing decisions. Everyone can decide what kind of ecological impact they are ready to accept each time they make a purchase.[207]

By thinking about our carbon footprint, we are encouraged to understand the overall effect of individual products or services on the environment and to make production more transparent. However, often the consumer is reduced to making sense of various logos and descriptions on the product itself. This can be confusing, and in the end, doesn't mean that the product was made sustainably. The possibility of integrating bar code (or QR code) information has already been explored to show supply chains, but like many innovations in this field, it has not been rolled out on a broad scale.

B Developments

Going beyond growth

Can we imagine the end of growth? The point where we say, we are big enough? The post-growth economy is one of the basic ideas for challenging our addiction to growth. This theory breaks with the idea that hunger, poverty, or distributive justice can only be compensated for by economic expansion. It's particularly useful when we look at the explosive increases in demand in nations such as China and India.[208]

A similar approach is the steady state economy — an economy whose state has reached an optimal level. From this point on, it will no longer grow physically, but will continue to develop at a sustainable consumption level and with a constant population.

The de-growth concept takes things one step further. Born from growth-critical debates, de-growth describes a reduction in consumption and production and thus a decline in GDP. Proponents of this more radical concept see it as a path to more social justice, environmental sustainability, and well-being.[209]

One area where these ideas can be easily applied is in agriculture. Seasonal and organic foods are produced at the regional level, with funding organized in solidarity, depending on who has more or fewer financial resources available. Consumers and producers take decisions jointly to reduce waste or environmental impact. One real-world example of this approach is the German organization 'Kauf ne Kuh' (Buy a Cow https://www.kaufnekuh.de), where consumers can order locally farmed meat on a shared basis. The cows for sale are displayed on the website, and together with others consumers, one can purchase a part of the chosen cow. Only when the whole cow is bought is it slaughtered. As such, the customer has direct contact with the product they consume and reduces waste by ordering collectively. The concept of collective enterprises works in a similar fashion. Such companies produce in an eco-friendly way and distribute the revenue as evenly as possible to their employees.[210]

So far, these concepts haven't been tested in practice. However, the post-growth economy will gradually be taken up by the sharing economy. Car sharing, municipal washing centers, or tool-sharing offer an alternative to ownership and thereby reduce consumption. Sharing saves resources — this is a key element of the post-growth economy.[211] Related to this approach is the green economy, which is promoted by politics.[212] There are many best practices where the green approach is integrated into a business model. Take Patagonia, the US outdoor clothing manufacturer: The company reports its environmental impact and the conditions in its research laboratories, and launches sustainability initiatives.[213] On the consumer side, there are numerous initiatives which challenge companies to take action to be sustainable. Third-party product reviews are playing an increasingly important role in this respect.[214] An example is provenance.org,[215] which tracks and verifies the origin of various products.

Fundamental behavioral change towards sustainable consumption

We must make our consumption more sustainable. But who is responsible for this? The current prevailing conviction is: "He who buys decides." Consumers have the power, and thus the responsibility, to influence production practices. Consumption is therefore a moral question. Faced with this sometimes overwhelming responsibility, many people flee into symbolic acts, such as small donations or CO^2 offset payments for flights. However, fundamental changes in consumer behavior are rare, on the one hand for financial reasons, and on the other because the goal remains abstract. The social benefit is not directly apparent in the present, but rather is aimed at avoiding future damage.[216]

The responsibility of the consumers

The concept of an empowered and responsible consumer presupposes that he or she is supported by product transparency and corresponding offers. However, in reality, this is often not the case. Research has shown that unclear information about a product's origins, lack of transparency in manufacturing conditions, lack of sustainable alternatives, and high prices all prevent people from consuming sustainably.[217]

The responsibility of companies

Part of the responsibility lies with the companies. It is up to them to not take advantage of the consumer dilemma, but to support them in their decision. Companies must first be transparent about their products.[218] Second, they must ensure that all stakeholders have common values, in order to ultimately add value to the society and the company itself.[219] In order for companies to seriously integrate such concepts into their business models, external pressure is needed, for example from politics.

Growth as a cycle

As long as the sustainable use of goods is limited to a niche market, there is a risk of greenwashing.[220] In order to achieve significant effects, it is necessary, however, for companies to examine their entire supply chain for opportunities to increase sustainability. In addition to product transparency, sustainable resources and land use, fair trade partnerships and cooperation are needed.[221]

Change starts with every one of us. Next time you go to the supermarket or department store, pay attention to which products you buy and which companies you support.

Take the train for short distance business trips. You won't waste time checking in, going through security, and boarding, and you can work while you ride.

Share, don't own. Make sharing services easily accessible to your employees. Open a business account at a ride-share company. Car-sharing works well in major cities; bike-sharing is often available as well and lets you get your daily exercise while commuting to work and meetings.

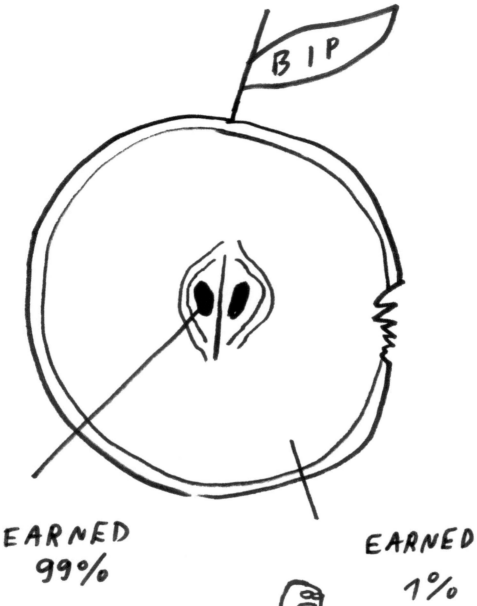

Text: Raquel Dischinger, Monika Smith

A Status

Well-being as a key word for prosperity

Sometimes contradictions which are barely noticeable on a large scale suddenly become apparent on a small one. "How are you doing?" and "How is the company turnover?" are some examples of the different personal questions we ask. On the other hand, when it comes to entire economies, we have long pretended that the two questions basically mean the same thing. For decades, the gross domestic product (GDP) was the most important measure of a country's economic state.

This is now changing. There is a growing realization that the question must actually be: How are the people who live in the country?

Well-being has become a key word when it comes to wealth and sustainable development.[222] As early as the 1980s, Amartya Sen, Nobel laureate in economics, developed holistic welfare standards. With the capability approach, he provided an alternative to welfare economics that well-being goes along with either wealth or profits. A core concept, which he also discussed extensively in his work Development as Freedom (1999),[223] is that the goal of social development and progress must be to increase the opportunities and freedoms of people.[224] Sen's structure is the basis of numerous United Nations' projects.

Since the year 2000, the Organization for Economic Co-operation and Development (OECD) has also been concerned with finding better and more comprehensive indicators for the progress of societies than GDP. The result is the World Happiness Report, which the organization has been publishing since 2012, and which is intended to measure global well-being. The 2017 UN report emphasizes the social foundations of happiness and discourages using GDP as the sole measure of well-being.[225] Numerous factors are included in such calculations.

Inequality is growing nationally and shrinking internationally

Another important measure to describe the state of the world is social inequality. People can participate in society and partake of its resources very differently. This goes beyond economic aspects to include, for example, political participation.[226]

As global inequality decreases, inequality is an ever more significant problem in many countries. According to the IMF, income inequality has increased in 53 percent of countries over the past three decades. This trend is particularly pronounced in developed economies. High levels of personal debt, coupled with inadequate savings and pension provisions, suggests that these problems will be exacerbated in the coming years.[227]

According to the report "Reward Work, not Wealth," published by the NGO Oxfam shortly before the World Economic Forum in Davos, 82 percent of the wealth generated in 2017 went to the richest 1 percent of the world's population. In other words, the richest 1 percent of the world's population has more wealth than the other 99 percent combined. In 2002, the proportion was 43 percent. According to Oxfam, this development will not be curbed by the fact that incomes in China, other Asian countries, and Latin America are growing faster than in the richest countries.[228] This inequality and low social mobility have aroused legitimate anger that our systems are designed to favor a handful of elites.

While distribution within individual states tends to become less equal, it is evolving globally for the better. Poverty and inequality have decreased significantly since the turn of the millennium. In 2001, nearly 30 percent of the world's population was poor and had to live on less than $2 a day. Within a decade, that number was halved, as shown in an evaluation by the Pew Research Center. Average incomes have also grown significantly more than top incomes, thus reducing global inequality.[229]

B Developments

The universal basic income

A further development of these mechanisms is the universal basic income (UBI). In the future, an ever-decreasing proportion of human labor will continue to support the traditional value chain.[230]

Advocates of a UBI hope for more freedom and security for every member of society. Especially with regard to the consequences of digitization and automation, a guaranteed income could counteract the feared mass unemployment and reduce the risk of poverty.[231] In addition, it is hoped that a UBI would increase work motivation and performance, since people would have the opportunity to work and live the way they have always wanted to — spending more time with family, becoming involved in society, or planning recovery periods. What has often been dismissed as a utopian thought experiment can give us the opportunity to completely rethink work; and for entrepreneurs, the question will be how they handle it.

Preserving democratic values

If we want to measure the prosperity of our society more than the sum of our income, then we realize that fair distribution does not only refer to money. Political participation, for example, is unevenly distributed in all Western democracies, depending to a large extent on education and income. People with low educational levels and low incomes are much less likely to participate in policy-making.[232]

Inequality through technology

Automation could further increase inequality — but only if we do not shape it. According to some research, automation and digitization will decrease overall employment and wages, while income and wealth will be increased.[233] By 2020, automation may eliminate around 20 to 25 percent of current jobs, hitting middle- to low-income workers the hardest.[234] This does not automatically mean that those people will be unemployed. Forecasts estimate that around 300 million people worldwide will be professionally reoriented by 2030 due to automation.[235]

Digital technologies can certainly exacerbate inequalities. One example can be found in human resources. In the US, it is common for workers to know the creditworthiness of an employee and to use reviews on Facebook, Twitter, or LinkedIn for hiring decisions.[236] Manipulation is nothing new, but in recent years the impact through automatization has grown tremendously. Hacking the human brain has swiftly progressed, even making it possible to target people based on their individual preferences, be they ads clicked, products bought, or politicians voted for. The outlook is daunting – in just a few years, biometric sensors could give human hackers an insight into our bodies and our soul, monitoring our mood and emotions and drawing connections with other data, like our spending history, clicks and channel subscriptions.[237]

In order to prevent such scenarios, it is necessary to be sure of your values and identity. Transformation starts by knowing your why, how and what. To understand the current economical, ecological, societal, cultural and technological developments and their interdependencies. Now it is up to you get active, connect the dots and create a positive impact in our world.

Happiness of employees is an imperative in business. Foster meaningful relationships. According to Harvard Business Review, close work friendships lift employee satisfaction by 50 percent.[238] Implement this knowledge into your team building efforts and create opportunities for your team members to meet and get to know each other. This can be done with a regular team event like a brunch meeting every month, or team weekends where you offer team building and free time, as well as on a daily basis by enabling team members to meet when making their coffee in an inviting coffee kitchen or having lunch together.

Create a value pyramid for your company's culture. Hold an interactive workshop to build your value pyramid. This is not only a very effective team building event, but also extremely valuable for aligning your company values to the values of individuals in your company. By identifying what's important to the individual and the team, they will have a better understanding of how to motivate themselves in their role and get inspired. Try to work as visually as possible by creating a poster or sculpture, and make it accessible after its completion so that people can look at it. Once you have your team pulling together on a project, specific task, or company goal, your shared value pyramid acts as a catalyst for further motivation and enables future innovation.

Know yourself. Learn about weakness and individual capabilities. Hire a red team to get a full vulnerability report. That combined is the best prevention against human hacking.

appendix

Why Are You Unhappy?
(Wei Wu Wei)

"Why are you unhappy?
Because 99.9 per cent
Of everything you think,
And of everything you do,
Is for yourself –
And there isn't one."

Acknowledgements

A lot of experts contributed to the creation of this book. I'm thanking all authors, co-authors, challengers and research contributors. Through your expertise and efforts we created a tangible source for purpose design – with multiple perspectives and from various backgrounds.

Authors

Dr. Maren Beverung, Scot Carlson, Pascal Fantou, Curt Simon Harlinghausen, Daniel Heltzel, Steffan Heuer, Philip Siefer, Martin Sinner, Christian Solmecke, Don Spampinato, Dr. Shermin Voshmgir, Katharina Zwielich

Co–Authors

Amrei Andrasch, Jean-Philip Almstedt, Victoria Balk, Jannis Born, Raquel Dischinger, Tina Dreisicke, Dominik Frisch, Jukka Hilmola, Robin Jadkowski, Nimrod Lehavi, Marcus Prosch, Long Qu, Mats Richter, Friederike Rohde, Stefan Pfeifer, Romas Stukenberg, Maximilian Wächter, Maximilian Weldert, Magdalena Witty, Nicole Wohltran

I'm grateful, as well, to the professionals who volunteered as mentors, challenging each and every article, and discussing them further. Without the time they generously offered, I couldn't have written this book.

Lukas Pardylla and Jan Stassen from the Co-Creation Loft Berlin, for all their insights on the topic of innovation space. The cognitive scientist Ngan-Tram Ho Da for her support with the workshop set-up and her mentoring in the area of Planet. Kilian Frühauf, partner at the holistic consultancy Summer & Co for his support in the area of Organizational Development. Marek Spak for his mentoring in the area of Technology as well as Svenja Bickert-Appleby for her support in the area of Culture. And Manjot Bhatia, Partner at Journey and Creation for his mentoring overall.

Furthermore I owe a big thank you to the editors Alexander Langer, Christoph Koch, Antje Dohmann, Martin Mühl, Jennifer Giwi and Jakob von Lindern as well as, Peta Jenkin and Madeleine LaRue for the edit of the English version.

For the outstanding visual translation skills of the graphic recording duo Johanna Benz and Tiziana Jil Beck. They captured our discussions, thoughts, ideas and visions in real time with nothing other than active listening, pen and paper.

Furthermore the incredible T.S. Wendelstein and his Studio The Simple Society, who gave this project its visual language and the book its design and layout. With it a special thanks to Malwine Stauss for the plentiful hours of layout work.

Thanks to my dear friend Ute Schechtel, a creative spirit with a big heart. As a facilitator in numerous discussions, you integrated the human dimension again and again into our thinking and challenged, encouraged and activated me. Of course a big thanks to my friends Dominik Heilig and Chiara Hummel, who always had time for motivating me or were simply there.

I also want to thank my mentor Iris von Tiedemann for her constant support and inspiration.

Above all, thank you Curt Simon Harlinghausen. He is not just sharing his knowledge as a co-author, but had an open ear and keen eyes for conceptual issues at any time in most remote places of the world. Hats off to your energy, your thinking and the exponential good willing beyond your doing. You are truly inspiring.

A book needs time, freedom and a critical eye or two. And brings along deadlines, night shifts and in one way or another creative obstacles. Please explain that to a four-year-old! A huge THANK YOU to my son Leino, who accompanied me with patience and curiosity. You are the future. And a major part of my purpose.

Thank you.

References

1

Bernardis, Alexander; Hochreiter, Gerhard; Lang, Matthias; Mitterer, Gerald "Purpose River" http://www.harvardbusinessmanager.de/blogs/a-1074239.html, 13.10.2018

2

Deutsche UNESCO-Kommission, "Erklärung von Mexico-City über Kulturpolitik. Weltkonferenz über Kulturpolitik", 1982, https://www.unesco.de/sites/default/files/2018-03/1982_Erkl percentC3 percen-tA4rung_von_ Mexiko.pdf > 05.03.2018.

3

https://www.openpetition. de/petition/online/erklaerung-zur-foer-derung-der-kultur-in-einer-sich-wandelnden-gesellschaft > 05.03.2018.

4

https://www.bbc.com/news/uk-scotland-44296386, 10.10.2018

5

According to the 2014 Meat Atlas of the Friends of the Earth and the Heinrich Böll Foundation.

6

Kaeser, Eduard, "Leben in Technotopia", in: agora42, 02/2017, S. 9.

7

Lotter, Wolf, "Die Selbstbestimmer", in: brand eins 01/2015, S. 46.

8

Ibid., S. 47

9

Stadler, Felix, "Grundformen der Digitalität", in: agora42 02/2017, S. 24 – 27.

10

Gill, Bernhard, "Nichtwissen in der postsäkularen Wissensgesell-schaft – Der Zuwachs an selbstdefiniertem und fremddefiniertem Nichtwissen", 2004, https://epub.ub.uni-muenchen.de/13904/1/gill_13904.pdf > 03.05.2018.

11

Poltermann, Andreas, "Wissensgesellschaft – eine Idee im Realitäts-check", 2013, http://www.bpb.de/gesellschaft/kultur/zukunft-bil-dung/146199/wissensgesellschaft?p=0 > 27.04.2018.

12

Knoblauch, Hubert, "Wissenssoziologie, Wissensgesellschaft und die Transformation der Wissenskommunikation", 2013, http://www.bpb.de/apuz/158653/wissenssoziologie-wiss

13

Wessely, Uli, "Politische Bildung in der globalen Wissensge-sell-schaft", 2004, http://www.bpb.de/apuz/28522/politi-sche-bil-dung-in-der-globalen-wissensgesellschaft?p=all > 22.02.2018.

14

Lotter, Wolf, "Das neue Wir", 2016, https://www.brandeins.de/magazine/brand-eins-wirtschaftsmagazin/2016/wir/das-neue-wir > 22.02.2018.

15

Vinge, Vernor, "Signs of the Singularity. Hints of the singularity's approach can be found in the arguments of its critics", 2008, https://spectrum.ieee.org/biomedical/ethics/signs-of-the-singularity 27.04.2018.

16

Seeley, Thomas D, "Honeybee Democracy", October 10, 2010.

17

"New hope for humans in an A.I. world | Louis Rosenberg | TEDxKC", Youtube-Video von TEDx Talks, 2017, https://www.youtube.com/watch?v=Eu-RyZt_Uas > 19.03.2018.

18

Hanson, Robin, "Economics of the Singularity. Stuffed into skyscra-pers by the billion, brainy bugbots will be the knowledge workers of the future", 2008, https://spectrum.ieee.org/robotics/robotics-soft-ware/economics-of-the-singularity > 27.04.2018.

19

Hess, Peter, "Unanimous A.I. Uses Human Swarms to Make Scary-Accurate Predictions", https://www.inverse.com/ar-ticle/34696-unanimous-ai-human-swarm-unu > 03.10.2018.

20

Ibid.

21

Stadler, Felix, "Grundformen der Digitalität", in: agora42, 02/2017, S. 24 ff.

22

Lefrancois, G. R., "Psychologie des Lernens", 1994.
Stangl, Werner, Werner Stangls Arbeitsblätter, Onlinequelle: http://arbeitsblaetter.stangl-taller.at/LERNEN/, 2018 > 04.02.2018.

23

Caring Economics, "From Homo Economicus towards a Caring Economics", o. J., http://www.caring-economics.org/about > 25.04.2018.

24

Goihl, Katja, "Transformationale Führung, Implikationen für die ler-nende Verwaltung", als Dissertation im Fachbereich Erziehungs-wissenschaft und Psychologie der Freien Universität Berlin, 2003, S. 24
Argyris Chris/Schön Donald A., "Die Lernende Organisation", 2. Auflage. Stuttgart, 2002, S. 9

25

Hofbauer, Erika,: "Was Hänschen nicht lernt, wird Hans lernen müs-sen. Eine Wissensgesellschaft muss die Bereitschaft zum lebenslan-gen Lernen haben", in Wissenplus, Heft 3, 2007/08, S. 7.

26

Marsick, Victoria J. /Watkins, Karen E. "Demonstrating the Value of an Organization's Learning Culture: The Dimensions of the Learning. Organization questionnaire, Advances in Developing Human Resour-ces", 2003, 5, S. 132.

27

Zinth, Claas-Philip, "Organisationales Lernen als Lernweg des Subjekts",REPORT Zeitschrift für Weiterbildungsforschung, 33. Jahrgang, Heft 2/2010, 2010, S. 65.

28

Poltermann, Andreas "Wissensgesellschaft – eine Idee im Reali-täts-check", 2013, http://www.bpb.de/gesellschaft/kultur/zukunft-bil-dung/146199/wissensgesellschaft?p=0 > 27.04.2018.

29

arbeitsblaetter.stangl-taller.at/LERNEN/, 2018 > 4.2.2018.
46 Udacity, https://de.udacity.com/ > 04.02.2018

30

47 E-Teaching, "MOOCs – Hintergründe und Didaktik, Onlinequelle": https://www.e-teaching.org/lehrszenarien/mooc, 2018 > 04.02.2018.

31

Future (2017): "Virtual Reality, in: future – Das Zukunftsmagazin der Wiener Zeitung " (Ausgabe 1/2017), https://austria-forum.org/af/AEIOU/Virtual_Reality8 > 04.02.2018.

32

Kirschner, Femke/Paas, Fred/Kirschner, Paul A., "A cognitive load approach to collaborative learning: United brains for complex tasks", Educational Psychology Review, 21, 2009, S. 31-42.

33
Benjamin, David, "Rohstoffe der Zukunft – Wissen in der Cloud managen und sichern", https://www.pcwelt.de/ratgeber/Rohstoff-der-Zukunft-Wissen-in-der-Cloud-managen-und-sichern-10084295.html, 2017 > 09.02.2018

34
Jones, Nikola, "Wie Maschinen lernen lernen, " http://www.spektrum.de/news/maschinenlernen-deep-learning-macht-kuenstliche-intelligenz-praxistauglich/1220451, 2014 > 9.2.2018

35
Mathworks, "Deep learning – Drei Dinge, die Sie wissen sollten", https://de.mathworks.com/discovery/deep-learning. html > 04.02.2018.

36
Bersin, Josh, " 5 Keys to Building a Learning Organization", https://www.forbes.com/sites/joshbersin/2012/01/18/5-keys-to-building-a-learning-organization/#13ce0bef129c > 9.2.2018.

37
Lotter, Wolf, "Das neue Wir", 2016, https://www.brandeins.de/magazine/brand-eins-wirtschaftsmagazin/2016/wir/das-neue-wir > 21.02.2018.

38
https://de.wikipedia.org/wiki/Margaret_Mead > 05.05.2018.

39
World Economic Forum, "Global Gender Gap Report", 2017, https://www.weforum.org/reports/the-global-gender-gap-report-2017.

40
https://leanin.org/ > 05.09.2018.

41
https://editionf.com/ > 05.09.2018.

42
Ernst&Young GmbH, Charta der Vielfalt e.V., "Diversity in Deutschland. Studie anlässlich des 10-jährigen Bestehens der Charta der Vielfalt", 2016, https://www.charta-der-vielfalt.de/fileadmin/user_upload/Studien_Publikationen_Charta/STUDIE_DIVERSITY_IN_DEUTSCHLAND_2016-11.pdf, S. 25.

43
https://www.bcorporation.net/ > 05.05.2018.

44
Ernst&Young GmbH, Charta der Vielfalt e. V., "Diversity in Deutschland. Studie anlässlich des 10-jährigen Bestehens der Charta der Vielfalt", 2016, https://www.charta-der-vielfalt.de/fileadmin/user_upload/Studien_Publikationen_Charta/STUDIE_DIVERSITY_IN_DEUTSCHLAND_2016-11.pdf, S. 73.

45
Biniok, Peter, "Emanzipierende Infrastrukturen. Wie digitale Teilhabe ausgebaut werden kann", 2017, https://www.rosalux.de/fileadmin/rls_uploads/pdfs/Standpunkte/Standpunkte_9-2017.pdf, S. 2ff > 27.02.2018.

46
Leserbrief: "Ich will arbeiten, nicht mehr ein Mensch zweiter Klasse sein...", in: Hamburger Abendblatt, 2007, https://www.abendblatt.de/hamburg/von-mensch-zu-mensch/article107213577/Ich-will-arbeiten-nicht-mehr-ein-Mensch-zweiter-Klasse-sein.html > 18.03.2018.

47
Siegrist, Johannes, "The effort-reward imbalance model. Occupational Medicine", in: State of the Art Reviews, 15(1), 2000, S. 83 – 87.

48
Eichhorst, Werner, "Do we have to be afraid of the future world of work?", in: IZA Policy Paper, Nr. 102, 2015, S. 12.

49
Manyika, James u. a., "Jobs Lost, Jobs Gained: Workforce Transitions in a time of automation", McKinsey Global Institute, 2017, https://www.mckinsey.com/~/media/McKinsey/Global percent20Themes/Future percent20of percent20Organizations/What percent20the percent20future percent20of percent20 work percent20will percent20mean percent20for percent20jobs percent20skills percent20and percent20wages/MGI-Jobs-Lost-Jobs-Gained-Report-December-6-2017.ashx, S. vi > 28.04.2018.

50
Depireux, Philipp, "Ist das Grundeinkommen die Antwort auf den digitalen Arbeitsmarkt", in: Die Welt, 2018, https://www.welt.de/wirtschaft/bilanz/article168595016/Ist-das-Grundeinkommen-die-Antwort-auf-den-digitalen-Arbeitsmarkt.html > 29.04.2018.

51
Eichhorst, Werner, "Do we have to be afraid of the future world of work?", in: IZA Policy Paper, Nr. 102, 2015, S. 10.

52
Bauer, Georg F./Hämmig, Oliver, "Bridging Occupational, Organizational and Public Health. A Transdisciplinary Approach", Springer: Dordrecht u.a., 2014, https://doi.org/10.1007/978-94-007-5640-3, S. 9 > 02.05.2018.

53
Botthof, Alfons/Hartmann, Ernst A. (Hrsg.), "Zukunft der Arbeit in Industrie 4.0.", Springer Berlin, Heidelberg, 2015, https://doi.org/10.1007/978-3-662-45915-7, S. 49 > 02.05.2018.

54
Exner, Alexander u. a., "Selbststeuerung von Unternehmen: Ein Handbuch für Manager und Führungskräfte", Frankfurt, New York, 2009, S. 17.

55
Bain & Company, "Das Unternehmen der Zukunft ist selbstorganisiert und vernetzt", 2017, http://www.bain.de/press/press-archive/The_firm_of_the_future_is_self-organized_and_networked.aspx > 04.05.2018.

56
Oesterreich, Bernd, "Verbunden im Konsent – Was ist Soziokratie?", 2015, https://intrinsify.me/verbunden-im-konsent-was-ist-soziokratie/ > 29.04.2018.

57
Bain & Company, "Bain Studie über die Firma von morgen", 2017, http://www.bain.de/press/press-archive/The_firm_of_the_future_is_self-organized_and_networked.aspx > 18.05.2018.

58
Humphrey, Nicholas, "Seeing Red. A Study in Consciousness", Cambridge, Massachusetts, 2008, S. 98.

59
Dewey, John, "Die Erneuerung der Philosophie", Hamburg, 1989, S. 240f

60
Zeuch, Andreas, "Holacracy. Vom Scheitern eines Betriebssystems", 2016, http://www.unternehmensdemokraten.de/holacracy-vom-scheitern-eines-betriebssystems/ > 26.04.2018.

61
Vgl. Schulenburg, Nils, "Führung einer neuen Generation – Wie die Generation Y führen und geführt werden sollte", 2016.

62
Wolf, Andreas, "Entfaltend führen. Grundzüge einer Führungstheorie für das Komplexitätszeitalter", Masterarbeit an der Otto-von-Guericke-Universtät Magdeburg, 2013, beit an der Otto-von-Guericke-Universtät Magdeburg, 2013, https://d-nb.info/1130704378/34, S. 13 > 28.04.2018.

63
Berg, Justin M./Wrzesniewski, Amy/Dutton, Jane E., "Perceiving and responding to challenges in job crafting at different ranks", in: Journal of Organizational Behavior, Nr.31, 2010, S. 158 u. 165.

64
Wienecke, Patrick, "Resonanz: Der Schlüssel zur Welt", 2016, https://www.zukunftsinstitut.de/artikel/resonanz-der-schluessel-zur-welt/ > 03.03.2018.

65
Ryan, Liz, "Seven Leadership Skills Most Managers Lack", 2016, https://www.forbes.com/sites/lizryan/2016/05/26/seven-leadership-skills-most-managers-lack/#56c136a37ebb > 02.05.2018.

66
Hofert, Svenja, "Ich-Entwicklung für Führungskräfte. Warum Reife entscheidend ist", in: Huffington Post Deutschland, 2016, https://www.huffingtonpost.de/svenja-hofert/ichentwicklung-fuer-fuehr_b_11925114.html > 02.05.2018.

67
Weibler, Prof. Dr. Jürgen, "Bescheidenheit ist machtvoll – Führung durch Haltung", 2018, https://www.leadership-insiders.de/bescheidenheit-ist-machtvoll-fuehrung-durch-haltung/ > 03.05.2018.

68
22 Gloger, Boris, "Selbstorganisation braucht Führung", 2017, S.94; Lotter, Wolf, "Gute Arbeit", in: brand eins, Nr. 3, 2017, S. 33.

69
Greiner, Lena, "New Work. So haben die Millennials die Arbeitswelt verändert", in: Karriere Spiegel, 2018, http://www.spiegel.de/karriere/generation-y-so-haben-die-millennials-die-arbeitswelt-bereits-veraendert-a-1195595.html > 03.03.2018.

70
Budds, Diana, "Ideo's CEO On How To Lead An Organization Creatively", 2016, https://www.fastcodesign.com/3059787/ideos-ceo-on-how-to-lead-an-organization-creatively > 12.02.2018.

71
Williamson, Cheryl, "Servant Leadership: How To Put Your People Before Yourself", in: Forbes, Nr., 2017. https://www.forbes.com/sites/forbescoachescouncil/2017/07/19/servant-leadership-how-to-put-your-people-before-yourself/#2ed6d65a66bc > 26.02.2018.

72
Petrie, Nick, "Future Trends in Leadership Development" 2011, https://www.ccl.org/wp-content/uploads/2015/04/futureTrends.pdf S. 6 > 12.02.2018.

73
"Paul English built a unique culture at Kayak that was the foundation of that company's success. The founders created a system where their company culture of excellence and productivity was created from the hiring process through to operations. Meetings where decisions were to be made were to have no more than three people because then people were wasting their time. This created a culture of action and accountability while trading off consensus.", in: Ducker, Peter, "Culture Eats Strategy For Breakfast", 2014, https://techcrunch.com/2014/04/12/culture-eats-strategy-for-breakfast/ > 25.03.2018.

74
Sagmeister, Simon, "Business Culture Design. Gestalten Sie Ihre Unternehmenskultur mit der Culture Map", 2016. S. 36

75
Reeves, Martin, " Die Another Day: What Leaders Can Do About the Shrinking Life Expectancy of Corporations",2015, https://www.bcg.com/publications/2015/strategy-die-another-day-what-leaders-can-do-about-the-shrinking-life-expectancy-of-corporations.aspx > 05.03.2018

76
Lehnert, Benedikt, "The Open Design Review as a tool to establish a company-wide design culture", http://www.benedikt-lehnert.de/blog/open-design-reviews-as-a-tool-to-establish-a-company-wide-design-culture > 03.05.2018.

77
Ibid.

78
Guidice, Maria/Ireland, Christopher, "Rise of the DEO. Leadership by Design", 2013, S. 15.

79
http://stemtosteam.org > 03.05.2018.

80
van Dijk, Menno/Davidson, Grant/Mecozzi, Valeria, "What is Creative Leadership?", 2017, https://www.thnk.org/insights/what-is-creative-leadership/ > 03.05.2018.

81
https://page-online.de/branche-karriere/was-ist-eigentlich-strategisches-design// > 04.04.2018.

82
Lehnert, Benedikt, "The Open Design Review as a tool to establish a company-wide design culture", http://www.benedikt-lehnert.de/blog/open-design-reviews-as-a-tool-to-establish-a-company-wide-design-culture > 03.05.2018.

83
Ibid..

84
Olins, Wally, "The Shape of Brands to Come", 2014, S. 102 ff.

85
Lockwood, Thomas/Walton, Thomas, "Building Design Strategy. Using Design to Achieve Key Business Objectives", 2008, S. 3. Lockwood, Thomas, "Design Value: A Framework for Measurement", in: Design Management Review, Bd. 18, Nr. 4, 2007, S. 90 – 97.

86
Speicher, Sandy, "CREATING INSTABILITY. The uncomfortable secret to creative success is ›disequilibrium‹", 2017, https://qz.com/1118085/the-uncomfortable-secret-to-creative-success-is-disequilibrium/ > 03.05.2018.

87
Wood, Gavin, "Playful Design", 2012, http://thecreativeexchange.org/activity/playful-design > 10.02.2018.

88
Dippel, Anne/Fizek, Sonia, "Playful Laboratories. The significance of games for knowledge production in the digital age", 2016, https://rke.abertay.ac.uk/ws/portalfiles/portal/8799490, S. 2.

89
Seemann, Silke, "Playful Organization: Organisationales Spielen", 2016, https://www.zukunftsinstitut.de/artikel/playfulness/playful-organization-organisationales-spielen/ > 10.02.2018.

90
Gray, Alex, "The 10 skills you need to thrive in the Fourth Industrial Revolution", 2016, https://www.weforum.org/agenda/2016/01/the-10-skills-you-need-to-thrive-in-the-fourth-industrial-revolution/ > 16.02.2018.

91
https://www.inc.com/natalie-nixon/3-easy-ways-to-exercise-your-brain-s-creativity.html > 17.02.2018.

92
Bärtle, Doris, "etventure Digital Transformation Study 2017: German companies are too slow and inflexible", 2017, https://www.etventure.com/blog/etventure-digital-transformation-study-2017-german-companies-are-too-slow-and-inflexible/ > 10.02.2018.

93
Genpact, "White Paper. Design Thinking innovation for business processes and operations. An overlooked key to growth, not just cost", 2017, http://www.genpact.com/downloadable-content/insight/design-thinking-innovation-for-business-processes-and-operations-an-overlooked-key-to-growth-not-just-cost.pdf, S. 4 > 31.01.2018

94
https://www.inc.com/natalie-nixon/3-easy-ways-to-exercise-your-brain-s-creativity.html > 17.02.2018.

95
Hauschildt Jürgen, Gemünden Hans Georg, "Dimensionen der Innovation", 2016 > S3, https://www.researchgate.net/profile/Hans_Gemuenden/publication/300360879_Dimensionen_der_Innovation/links/57e20c8808aed96fbbb0832d/Dimensionen-der-Innovation.pdf > 05.05.2018.

96
Weber, Susanne, "Innovation und ›schöpferische Zerstörung‹ (J.A. Schumpeter). Fragen zu einem Leitbegriff moderner ökonomischer Strategien", 2001, http://www.fernuni-hagen.de/PRPH/webinn. pdf, S. 1 ff.

97
Schumpeter, Joseph A., "Theorie der wirtschaftlichen Entwicklung", 1987, S. 132.; Borbély, Emese, "J. A. Schumpeter und die Innovationsforschung", 2008, https://kgk.uni-obuda.hu/sites/default/files/33_BorbelyEmese.pdf, S. 401 > 07.03.2018.

98
Link, Stefan, "Why Design Thinking is the Future of Management", 2017, https://medium.com/swlh/project-management-3-0-why-design-thinking-is-the-next-gen-5be78e509103 > 05.02.2018.

99
Ibid.
100
Ringel, Michael u. a., "The Rising Need for Innovation Speed", 2015, https://www.bcg.com/publications/2015/growth-lean-manufacturing-rising-need-for-innovation-speed.aspx > 31.01.2018.

101
Glessner, Dan, "Two key ingredients for success in digital age: Design thinking and rapid innovation", 2016, http://www.genpact.com/insight/blog/two-key-ingredients-for-success-in-digital-age-design-thinking-and-rapid-innovation > 31.01.2018.

102
Gronemeyer, Marianne, "Immer wieder neu oder ewig das Gleiche. Innovationsfieber und Wiederholungswahn", 2000, S. 6.

103
Morris, Langdon, "Speed of Innovation – How to Master Rapid Prototyping", 2015, http://www.innovationmanagement.se/2015/05/19/speed-of-innovation-how-to-master-rapid-prototyping/ > 31.01.2018.

104
Howaldt, Prof. Dr. Jürgen, "Soziale Innovation im Fokus nachhaltiger Entwicklung. Zukunftsfähige Entwicklung und generative Organisationskulturen", 2015, http://www.hochschule-bochum.de/fileadmin/media/izk/ZEGO/vortraege14_15/Vortrag-Howaldt-Sozialforschungsstelle.pdf, S. 6 > 31.01.2018.

105
Wheatley, Margaret J./Kellner-Rogers, Mylon, "Bringing Life to Organizational Change", 1998, http://www.margaretwheatley.com/articles/life.html > 06.02.2018.

106
Bartl, Michael, "Open Innovation. Der offene Umgang mit Wissen verändert das Innovationsmanagement", 2010, http://www.community-of-knowledge.de/beitrag/open-innovation-der-offene-umgang-mit-wissen-veraendert-das-innovations-management/ > 13.03.2018.

107
Nobel, Dennis, "Warum schnelles Prototyping in IoT-Projekten unerlässlich ist. Prototyping für das Internet of Things", 2018, https://entwickler.de/online/iot/prototyping-iot-579809933.html > 31.01.2018.

108
Arnautovic, Vedran, "Using Design Sprint to accelerate innovation (part I of II)", 2015, https://medium.com/seek-blog/using-design-sprint-to-accelerate-innovation-part-i-of-ii-f643ad42cf60 > 31.01.2018.

109
Ringel, Michael u. a., "The Rising Need for Innovation Speed", 2015, https://www.bcg.com/publications/2015/growth-lean-manufacturing-rising-need-for-innovation-speed.aspx > 31.01.2018. https://www.bcg.com/publications/2015/growth-lean-manufacturing-rising-need-for-innovation-speed.aspx > 11.03.2018.

110
Morris, Langdon, "Speed of Innovation – How to Master Rapid Prototyping", 2015, http://www.innovationmanagement.se/2015/05/19/speed-of-innovation-how-to-master-rapid-prototyping > 31.01.2018

111
Ibid.

112
Vaas, Rüdiger, "Emotionen", 2000, http://www.spektrum.de/lexikon/neurowissenschaft/emotionen/3405m > 08.03.2018.

113
DTALE Design Studio, "5 Ways Emotional Design can help your business grow", 2017, https://medium.com/productivity-revolution/5-ways-emotional-design-can-help-your-business-grow-f1dbe-031b30e > 08.02.2018.

114
Winnick, Michael, "Putting a Finger on Our Phone Obsession. Mobile touches: a study on humans and their tech", 2016, https://blog.dscout.com/mobile-touches > 03.05.2018.

115
Brueck, Hilary, "This is what your smartphone is doing to your brain – and it isn't good", 2018, http://www.businessinsider.com/what-your-smartphone-is-doing-to-your-brain-and-it-isnt-good-2018-3 > 03.05.2018

116
Khoi Vinh, IxDA-Berlin-Vortrag, 12.02.2018.

117
Timmer, Sjors, "A room for understanding. The dawn of a new workspace", 2017, https://uxdesign.cc/a-room-for-understanding-593ef6f8c76e > 14.02.2018.

118
Schwab, Klaus, "Don't underestimate the value of dialogue", 2018, https://www.weforum.org/agenda/2018/02/dont-underestimate-the-value-of-dialogue/?utm_content=buffera2b1d&utm_medium= social&utm_source=facebook.com&utm_campaign=buffer > 03.05.2018.

119
Weber, Susanne, "Innovation und ›schöpferische Zerstörung‹ (J.A. Schumpeter). Fragen zu einem Leitbegriff moderner ökonomischer Strategien", 2001, http://www.fernuni-hagen.de/PRPH/webinn. pdf, S. 1 ff.

120
Lotter, Wolf, "Das neue Wir", 2016, https://www.brandeins.de/magazine/brand-eins-wirtschaftsmagazin/2016/wir/das-neue-wir > 12.02.2018.

121
" Redefining Value, to Business and to Society by Nathan Shedroff from California College of the Arts", Youtube-Video des Service Design Network, 2014, https://www.youtube.com/watch?v=9pfqZWMpJJY > 03.05.2018

122
Irwin, Terry u. a., "Transition Design 2015. A new area of design research, practice and study that proposes design-led societal transition toward more sustainable futures", 2015, https://design. cmu.edu/sites/default/files/Transition_Design_Monograph_final.pdf, S. 1ff > 16.02.2018.

123
Woodward Ph. D., Michael, "How to Thrive in a VUCA World. The Psychology of Navigating Volatile, Uncertain, Complex, & Ambiguous Times", 2017, https://www.psychologytoday.com/blog/spotting-opportunity/201707/how-thrive-in-vuca-world > 14.02.2018. Nienkerke-Springer, Dr. Anke, "Bewältigungsstrategien für die Herausforderungen der Vuca-Welt", 2017, http://www.nienkerke-springer.de/bewaeltigungsstrategien-fuer-die-herausforderungen-der-vuca-welt.pdfx, S. 1 ff > 08.03.2018.

124
Krapf, Joël, "Was für eine Kultur braucht eine agile Organisation?", 2017, https://joel-krapf.com/2017/04/06/was-fuer-eine-kultur-braucht-eine-agile-organisation/ > 05.05.2018.

125
HRM-Redaktion, "Kulturbildung in Zeiten der Digitalisierung", 2016, http://www.hrm.de/fachartikel/peter-kruse:-kulturbildung-in-zeiten-der-digitalisierung--13761 > 09.03.2018.

126
Bhabha, Homi K., "Die Verortung der Kultur", 2000, S. 5.

127
Ricci, Frederick A., "CULTIVATING CRITICAL THINKING WITHIN ORGANIZATIONS", 2014, http://www.ocerint.org/Socioint14_ebook/papers/48.pdf, S. 67 > 12.02.2018.

128
Schwab, Klaus, "Don't underestimate the value of dialogue", 2018, https://www.weforum.org/agenda/2018/02/dont-underestimate-the-value-of-dialogue/?utm_content=buffera2b1d&utm_medium=social&utm_source=facebook.com&utm_campaign=buffer > 03.05.2018.

129
Wendt, Thomas, "TOWARD SUSTAINABLE DESIGN THINKING", 2017, http://www.thedesigngym.com/toward-sustainable-design-thinking/ > 14.02.2018.

130
https://www.lean.org/lexicon/jidoka > 09.09.2018

131
https://www.thebalance.com/optimize-end-to-end-supply-chain-4022954 > 09.09.2018

132
http://www.fundinguniverse.com/company-histories/amazon-com-inc-history/ > 09.09.2018

133
https://www.cnbc.com/2016/05/13/5-key-business-lessons-from-amazons-jeff-bezos.html > 09.09.2018

134
http://www.dmi.org/?DesignValue > 09.09.2018

135
https://medium.com/trendwatching-pulse/your-brand-was-a-black-box-now-its-a-glass-box-6e64269ce458 > 09.09.2018

136
http://learn.cspace.com/hubfs/C_Space_Reports/CQ17_Unlocking percent20Customer percent20Inspired percent20Growth_C percent20Space.pdf > 09.09.2018

137
http://www.hrreview.co.uk/hr-news/strategy-news/holacracy-pros-and-cons-of-a-radical-challenge-to-the-traditional-organisation/50404 > 09.09.2018

138
https://blog.holacracy.org/holacracy-vs-hierarchy-vs-flat-orgs-d1545d5dffa7 > 09.09.2018

139
https://www.kiro7.com/news/local/woman-says-her-amazon-device-recorded-private-conversation-sent-it-out-to-random-contact/755507974 > 29.09.2018

140
https://www.nytimes.com/2018/05/25/business/amazon-alexa-conversation-shared-echo.html > 29.09.2018

141
Mayer-Schönberger, Viktor/Ramge, Thomas, "Das Digital: Markt, Wertschöpfung und Gerechtigkeit im Datenkapitalismus", 2017.

142
https://www.seagate.com/our-story/data-age-2025/ > 08.03.2018.

143
DC White Paper, "Data Age 2025 – The Evolution of Data to Life-Critical" 2017 IDC, www.idc.com > 08.03.2018

144
Stevens August "Big Data and the Future of Qualitative Research", 2014, https://rwconnect.esomar.org/big-data-and-the-future-of-qualitative-research/ > 28.04.2018.

145
IDC White Paper, "Data Age 2025 – The Evolution of Data to Life-Critical" 2017 IDC, www.idc.com > 08.03.2018.

146
ADAC, "ADAC Untersuchung an vier Fahrzeugen – Welche Daten erzeugt ein modernes Auto?", o. J.,https://www.adac.de/infotestrat/technik-und-zubehoer/fahrerassistenzsysteme/daten_im_auto/default.aspx > 26.04.2018.

147
Pinker, Steven, "The language instinct: How the mind creates language", 2003.

148
http://www.udu.co/blog/whatever-machines-havent-done-yet > 26.04.2018

149
Marr, Bernhard, "What Is The Difference Between Artificial Intelli-gence And Machine Learning?", Forbes, 2016, https://www.forbes. com/sites/bernardmarr/2016/12/06/what-is-the-difference-between-artificial-intelligence-and-machine-learning/#29712a7b2742 > 26.04.2018.

150
Stringer, Simon, director of Oxford Centre for Theoretical Neuroscience and AI, University of Oxford, in: Kaminska, Izabella, "Since you asked: Awkward questions on AI", in: Financial Times, 2007, https://www.ft.com/content/4024ef7e-a596-11e5-a91e-162b86790c58 > 03.05.2018.

151
Bughin, Jacques, et al "Artificial Intelligence – The next digital frontier", McKinsey&Company, McKinsey Global Institute, 2017 > 03.05.2018.

152
Krizhevsky, Alex/Sutskever, Ilya/Hinton, Geoffrey E., "ImageNet classification with deep convolutional neural networks", NIPS, 2012, http://papers.nips.cc/paper/4824-imagenet-classification-with-deep-convolutional-neural-networks > 21.02.2018.

153
Goodfellow, Ian u. a., "Generative Adversarial Nets", NIPS, 27, 2014, https://papers.nips.cc/paper/5423-generative-adversarial-nets.pdf > 21.02.2018

154
o. V., "Artificial Intelligence Revenue to Reach $36.8 World-ld-wide by 2025", Tractica.com, 2016, https://www.tractica.com/newsroom/press-releases/artificial-intelligence-revenue-to-reach-36-8-billion-worldwide-by-2025/ > 28.04.2018.

155
Columbus, Luis, "McKinsey's State Of Machine Learning And AI, 2017", Forbes, 2017, https://www.forbes.com/sites/louiscolumbus/2017/07/09/mckinseys-state-of-machine-learning-and-ai-2017/#a5e34d675b64 > 28.04.2018.

156
Bughin, Jacques u. a., "Artificial Intelligence – The next digital fron-tier", McKinsey&Company, McKinsey Global Institute, 2017 > 26.04.2018.

157
The state of Artificial Intelligence", CB Insights, 2017, https://www.cbinsights.com/research/report/artificial-intelligence-trends/ > 28.04.2018

158
Bughin, Jacques u. a., "Artificial Intelligence – The next digital fron-tier", McKinsey&Company, 2017, > 26.04.2018.

159
The state of Artificial Intelligence", CB Insights, 2017, https://www.cbinsights.com/research/report/artificial-intelligence-trends/ > 28.04.2018.

160
Büst, Rene, "Das Fundament der Künstlichen Intelligenz" in T3n, 2017, Mai 2017, > https://t3n.de/magazin/kuenstliche-intelligenz-geschaeftsmodell-unternehmen-242783 > 28.04.2018.

161
https://singularitynet.io > 21.02.2018.

162
Lin, Patrick, "Why Ethics Matters for Autonomous Cars", in: Maurer Markus u. a., Autonomous Driving, 2016.

163
https://www.seagate.com/our-story/data-age-2025/ > 08.03.2018.
Van Wynsberghe, Aimee, "Designing robots for care: Care centered value-sensitive design", in: Science and engineering ethics, 19(2), 2013, S. 407 – 433.

164
Lin, Patrick, "Why Ethics Matters for Autonomous Cars", in: Maurer Markus u. a., Autonomous Driving, 2016.

165
Spiekermann, Sara, "Künstliche Intelligenz – mehr Fluch als Segen", Der Standard, 2016, derstandard.at/2000048339674/Kuenstliche-Intelligenz-Mehr-Fluch-als-Segen > 28.04.2018.

166
Marr, Bernhard, "The Biggest Challenges Facing Artificial Intelligen-ce (AI)", Business And Society, Forbes, 2017, https://www.forbes. com/sites/bernardmarr/2017/07/13/the-biggest-challenges-facing-artificial-intelligence-ai-in-business-and-society/#5f20ae642aec > 28.04.2018.

167
Litzel, Nico, "Definition Was ist das Industrial Internet of Things (IIOT)?", Big Data Insider, 2017, https://www.bigdata-insider.de/was-ist-das-industrial-internet-of-things-iiot-a-654986/ > 28.04.2018.

168
Cuffari, Benedette, "The Future of Sensor Technology in the Global Market", AZO-Sensors, 2017, https://www.azosensors.com/article.aspx?ArticleID=775 > 28.04.2018.

169
Simon, Walter, "Tektonische Verschiebungen in der Arbeitswelt Industrie 4.0 – Fertigung und IT wachsen zusammen", Computerwo-che Tech Workshop, 2013, https://www.tecchannel.de/a/industrie-4-0-fertigung-und-it-wachsen-zusammen,2043878,2 > 28.04.2018.

170
Hackmann, Joachim, "Internet of Things (IoT) in der Praxis Industrie 4.0 ist das Internet der Ingenieure", in: Computerwoche, https://www.computerwoche.de/a/industrie-4-0-ist-das-internet-der-ingenieure,2538117 > 28.04.2018.

171
Ibid.

172
o. V., "Consol beleuchtet kurz- und mittelfristige IoT-Trends", consol, 2017, https://www.consol.de/presse/presse-meldungen/details/consol-beleuchtet-kurz-und-mittelfristige-iot-trends/ > 28.04.2018.

173
Chavez-Dreyfuss, Gertrude, "Sweden tests Blockchain technology for land registry", Reuters, 2016, https://www.reuters.com/article/us-sweden-Blockchain/sweden-tests-Blockchain-technology-for-land-registry-idUSKCN0Z22KV > 28.04.2018

174
Althauser, Joshua. "Indian State Uses Blockchain Technology To Stop Land Ownership Fraud", Cointelegraph, 2017, https://cointelegraph.com/news/indian-state-uses-Blockchain-technology-to-stop-land-ownership-fraud > 28.04.2018. (Version vom 24.02.2018)

175
Schaltegger, Prof. Dr. Stefan, "Sustainable Entrepreneurship als Treiber von Transformation", 2017, http://www.zukunftsinstitut.de/artikel/sustainable-entrepreneurship-als-treiber-von-transformation/ > 21.04.2018.

176
Umweltbundesamt, "Energieverbrauch nach Energieträgern, Sek-to-ren und Anwendungen", 2018, https://www.umweltbundesamt.de/daten/energie/energieverbrauch-nach-energietraegern-sektoren > 22.04.2018.

177
Grefe, Christiane, "Digitalisierung. Der Stromhunger wächst", in: Zeit Online, 2018, http://www.zeit.de/2018/06/digitalisierung-klimaschutz-nachhaltigkeit-strombedarf/seite-2 > 23.04.2018.

178
Weißbuch Nachhaltigkeit, "Virtueller und materieller Ressourcenver-brauch", https://www.bevh.org/weissbuch-nachhaltigkeit/online-versandhandel/virtueller-und-materieller-ressourcenverbrauch/ > 21.04.2018.

179
Lange, Steffen/Santarius, Tillmann, "Smarte grüne Welt? Digitalisierung zwischen Überwachung, Konsum und Nachhaltig-keit", 2018

180
Umweltbundesamt, "Endenergieverbrauch und Energieeffizienz des Verkehrs", 06.04.2017, https://www.umweltbundesamt.de/daten/verkehr/endenergieverbrauch-energieeffizienz-des-verkehrs#textpart-1 > 21.04.2018.

181
Global Footprint Network, "You can't manage what you can't measu-re", 2018. https://www.footprintnetwork.org/ > 23.04.2018

182
trend:research und Leuphana Universität Lüneburg, "Definition und Marktanalyse von Bürgerenergie in Deutschland", 2013, https://www.unendlich-viel-energie.de/media/file/198.trendresearch_Definition_und_Marktanalyse_von_Buergerenergie_in_Deutschland_okt13..pdf > 21.04.2018.

183

9Plattform Digitale Energiewelt, "Grundsatzpapier der Plattform Digitale Energiewelt",S. 1, 2016, https://shop.dena.de/fileadmin/denashop/media/Downloads_Dateien/esd/9163_Grundsatzpapier_der_Plattform_Digitale_Energiewelt.pdf > 24.04.2018.

184

Vgl. Amin, S.M./Wollenberg, B. F. "Toward a Smart Grid Power Delivery for the 21st Century", in: IEEE Power Energy Magazine, Bd. 3, Nr. 5, 2005, S. 34 – 41. doi10.1109/MPAE.2005.1507024.

185

Energy Web Foundation, "Building the grid's digital DNA", http://energyweb.org/ > 21.04.2018.

186

We Power, https://wepower.network/ > 21.04.2018.

187

VDE-EGT, Verband der Elektrotechnik Elektronik Informations-tech-nik e. V., Energietechnische Gesellschaft im VDE, "VDE-Studie: Der Zellulare Ansatz. Grundlage einer erfolgreichen, regionenüberg-rei-fenden Energiewende", 2016.

188

Peter, Frank u. a., "Dezentralität und zellulare Optimierung – Auswir-kungen auf den Netzausbaubedarf", 2016

189

acatech, "Das Energiesystem resilient gestalten. Maßnahmen für eine gesicherte Versorgung",Stellungnahme Mai 2017, https://www.leopoldina.org/uploads/tx_leopublication/ESYS_Stellungnahme_Das_Energiesystem_resilient_gestalten.pdf > 25.04.2018.

190

Johnston, Stuart, "Blockchain at the Grid Edge", 13.04.2017, http://www.energynetworks.com.au/news/energy-insider/Block-chain-grid-edge > 21.04.2018.

191

Mayer, Berni, "Blockchain-Revolution im Energiesektor?", BTC-ECHO, 10.11.2017, https://www.btc-echo.de/Blockchain-revoluti-on-im-energiesektor/ > 21.04.2018.

192

Digiconomist, "Bitcoin Energy Consumption Index", 2018, https://digiconomist.net/bitcoin-energy-consumption > 21.04.2018.

193

Creyts, Jon/Trbovich, Ana, "Can Blockchain help us to address the world's energy issues?", World Economic Forum, 2018, https://www.weforum.org/agenda/2018/01/how-can-Blockchain-address-the-worlds-energy-issues/ > 22.04.2018.

194

Deutscher Bundestag, 18. Wahlperiode, "Drucksache 18/13304", 2017, http://dip21.bundestag.de/dip21/btd/18/133/1813304.pdf > 24.04.2018.

195

Kloth, Philipp, "Digitalisierung in der Energiewende und Wärmew-en-de", Energieheld Blog, 2016, https://www.energieheld.de/blog/digitalisierung-in-der-energiewende-und-waermewende/

196

Purcell, Sarah, "let us switch! how prepayment meters trap people in fuel poverty", Church Action on Poverty, 2014, http://www.church-poverty.org.uk/news/pressroom/resources/reports/letthemswitch > 26.04.2018.

197

Global Fashion Agenda & The Boston Consulting Group, "Pulse of the fashion industry", 2017, http://globalfashionagenda.com/wp-content/uploads/2017/05/Pulse-of-the-Fashion-Industry_2017.pdf > 21.04.2018.

198

Clean Clothes Campaign, 2018, https://cleanclothes.org/resources > 22.04.2018.

199

Global Fashion Agenda & BCG 2017 + Ellen MacArthur Foundati-on, McKinsey Center for Business and Environment & Stiftungsfonds für Umweltökonomie und Nachhaltigkeit (SUN), "Growth within. A circular economy vision for a competitive Europe", 2015, https://www.mckinsey.de/files/growth_within_report_circular_economy_in_europe.pdf > 21.04.2018.

200

Utopia, "Siegel-Guide", 2018, https://utopia.de/siegel-guide/ > 21.04.2018

201

CCCb, "Looking for a quick fix. How weak social auditing is keeping workers in sweatshops. Clean Clothes Campaign", 2005.

202

Herrigel, G./Voskamp, U./Wittke, V. "Globale Qualitätsprodukti-on. Transnationale Produktionssysteme in der deutschen Automobilzu-lieferindustrie und im Maschinenbau", 2017.

203

Ellen MacArthur Foundation, McKinsey Center for Business and Environment & Stiftungsfonds für Umweltökonomie und Nach-haltigkeit (SUN), "Growth within. A circular economy vision for a competitive Europe", 2015, https://www.mckinsey.de/files/growth_within_report_circular_economy_in_europe.pdf. S. 11 > 25.04.2018

204

Dietz, Rob/O'Neill, Dan, "Enough Is Enough. Building a Sustaina-ble Economy in a World of Finite Resources", 2013.

205

Club of Rome, https://www.clubofrome.org/report/the-limits-to-growth/, 2018 > 22.04.2018.

206

Bundesministerium für Umwelt, Naturschutz, Bau und Reaktor-si-cherheit, "Nachhaltiger Konsum", http://www.bmub.bund.de/themen/wirtschaft-produkte-ressourcen-tourismus/produkte-und-konsum/nachhaltiger-konsum/ > 21.04.2018.

207

Brand, Karl W., "Konsum im Kontext. Der ›verantwortliche Kon-su-ment‹ — ein Motor nachhaltigen Konsums?", in: Lange, Helmut (Hrsg.), "Nachhaltigkeit als radikaler Wandel",2008, https://link.springer.com/chapter/10.1007/978-3-531-90956-1_4 > 21.04.2018.

208

Paech, Niko, "Grundzüge einer Wachstumsökonomie", 2018, http://www.postwachstumsoekonomie.de/material/grundzuege/ > 21.04.2018.

209

IHK Nürnberg, "Postwachstum und Degrowth", Lexikon der Nach-haltigkeit, 2015, https://www.nachhaltigkeit.info/artikel/degrowth_1849.htm > 24.04.2018.

210

"Welche Unternehmen gibt es in der Postwachstumsöko-no-mie?", konzeptwerk neue ökonomie, 2013, https://www.konzept-werk-neue-oekonomie.org/welche-unternehmen-gibt-es-in-der-postwachstumsoekonomie/ > 21.04.2018.

211

Mont, Oksana, "Institutionalisation of sustainable consumption patterns based on shared use", in: Ecological Economics, Bd. 50, Nr. 1-2, 2004, https://doi.org/10.1016/j.ecolecon.2004.03.030, S. 135-153;

212

Umweltbundesamt, "Wirtschaft & Konsum", https://www.um-welt-bundesamt.de/themen/wirtschaft-konsum#strap1 > 21.04.2018.

213

Pönitzsch, Gert/Kniebes, Carola, "Proposal – Ways to achieve sus-tainable consumption", 2013, http://www.global-economic-sym-posium.org/knowledgebase/towards-sustainable-consumption/pro-posals/ways-to-achieve-sustainable-consumption > 26.04.2018.

214
Schaller, Stephan u. a., "Nachhaltigkeit in der deutschen Konsum-güterwirtschaft. Themen, Trends und Initiativen", 2012, https://www. gs1-germany.de/fileadmin/gs1/basis_informationen/Nachhaltigkeit_ in_der_Konsumgueterwirtschaft.pdf > 21.04.2018.

215
Provenance, 2018, https://www.provenance.org/how-it-works > 21.04.2018.

216
Balderjahn, Prof. Dr. Ingo, "Nachhaltiges Konsumverhalten", 2005, http://www.uni-potsdam.de/marketing_ls/dmdocuments/Praxis percent20und percent20Projekte/Vortraege/Balderjahn/vortrag_ nachhaltige.kon-sumstile_fu_31.01.05.pdf

Holzinger, Hans, "WACHSTUMSGRENZEN – DIE (POST-) WACHS-TUMSDEBATTE IN DER AKTUELLEN FACHLITERATUR", 2016, https://wachstumimwandel.at/wp-content/uploads/WiW-Dossier6_ Post_Wachstumsdebatte_web.pdf, S. 66.

217
Ahaus, Björn/Heidbrink, Ludger/Schmidt, Imke, "Der verantwortliche Konsumen. Wie Verbraucher mehr Verantwortung für ihren All-tagskonsum übernehmen können", Working Papers des CRR, 2011, http://www.responsibility-research.de/resources/WP_10_Der_ verantwortliche_Konsument+_.pdf > 25.04.2018.

218
Ahaus, Björn/Heidbrink, Ludger/Schmidt, Imke, "Der verantwortliche Konsumen. Wie Verbraucher mehr Verantwortung für ihren All-tagskonsum übernehmen können", Working Papers des CRR, 2011, http://www.responsibility-research.de/resources/WP_10_Der_ verantwortliche_Konsument+_.pdf > 25.04.2018.

219
Lexikon der Nachhaltigkeit, "Shared Value (Porter/Kramer)", 2015, https://www.nachhaltigkeit.info/artikel/shared_value_porter_ kramer_1946.htm > 21.04.2018.

220
Holzinger, Hans, "WACHSTUMSGRENZEN – DIE (POST-) WACHS-TUMSDEBATTE IN DER AKTUELLEN FACHLITERATUR", 2016, https://wachstumimwandel.at/wp-content/uploads/WiW-Dossier6_ Post_Wachstumsdebatte_web.pdf., S. 66 > 23.04.2018.

221
Schaller, Stephan u. a., "Nachhaltigkeit in der deutschen Konsum-güterwirtschaft. Themen, Trends und Initiativen", 2012, https://www. gs1-germany.de/fileadmin/gs1/basis_informationen/ Nachhaltigkeit_in_der_Konsumgueterwirtschaft.pdf > 23.04.2018.

222
Wikipedia, "Wohlbefinden", https://de.wikipedia.org/wiki/Wohlbefinden_(Wohlstandsindikator) > 07.04.2018.

223
Sen, A., "Development as freedom", 1999.

Digiconomist, "Bitcoin Energy Consumption Index", 2018, https://digiconomist.net/bitcoin-energy-consumption > 21.04.2018.

224
Wikipedia, "Wohlbefinden", https://de.wikipedia.org/wiki/ Wohlbefinden_(Wohlstandsindikator)#cite_note-3 > 22.04.2018.

225
62 Helliwell, John F./Layard, Richard/Sachs, Jeffrey D., "WORLD HAP-PINESS REPORT 2017", 2017 http://worldhappiness.report/ wp- content/uploads/sites/2/2017/03/HR17-Esv2_updated.pdf > 21.04.2018.

226
Welt-Sichten, "Ungleichheit kann die Demokratie gefährden. Agrar-reformen sind ein Weg, die soziale Kluft zu verkleinern", Gespräch mit Professor Hans-Jürgen Burchardt, 27.01.2008, https://www.welt-sichten.org/artikel/3849/ungleichheit-kann-die-demokratie-gefaehrden > 21.04.2018.

227
World Economic Forum, "Global Risks 2018: Fractures, Fears and Failures", http://reports.weforum.org/global-risks-2018/global- risks-2018-fractures-fears-and-failures/#view/fn-4 > 21.04.2018.

228
Obertreis, Rolf, "Oxfam-Studie. Soziale Ungleichheit nimmt weltweit drastisch zu", in: Der Tagesspiegel, 2018, http://www.tagesspiegel. de/wirtschaft/oxfam-studie-soziale-ungleichheit-nimmt-weltweit-drastisch-zu/20871368.html > 21.04.2018.

229
Stefan, Leopold, "Global betrachtet geht die soziale Kluft zu-rück", in: Der Standard, 15.02.2018, https://mobil.derstandard. at/2000074287961/Global-betrachtet-geht-die-soziale-Kluft- deut-lich-zurueck?utm_content=buffer7d05e&utm_medium= social&utm_ source=facebook.com&utm_campaign=buffer > 24.04.2018

230
Vollmer, Thomas u. a., "Digitale Vernetzung der Facharbeit: gewerb-lich-technische Berufsbildung in einer Arbeitswelt des Internets der Dinge", in: Berufsbildung, Arbeit und Innovation, Bd-Nr. 43 Reihe, Bielefeld, 2017, S. 43.

231
Eckert, Daniel, "Die Ängste der Deutschen erleben einen ›his-to-rischen Umschwung‹", in: Die Welt, 2017, https://www.welt.de/ wirtschaft/article168414060/Die-Aengste-der-Deutschen-erle-ben-einen-historischen-Umschwung.html > 26.04.2018.

232
Bödeker, Sebastian, "Die ungleiche Bürgergesellschaft – Warum so-ziale Ungleichheit zum Problem für die Demokratie wird", 13.08.2014, http://www.bpb.de/gesellschaft/kultur/zukunft-bildung/189941/ die-ungleiche-buergergesellschaft?p=all > 26.04.2018

233
World Economic Forum, "Global Risks 2018: Fractures, Fears and Failures", http://reports.weforum.org/global-risks-2018/ global-ris-ks-2018-fractures-fears-and-failures/#view/fn-4 > 22.04.2018.

234
Harris, Karen/Kimson, Austin/Schwedel, Andrew, "Labor 2030: The Collision of Demographics, Automation and Inequality. The business environment of the 2020s will be more volatile and economic swings more extreme", 2018, http://www.bain.de/Images/BAIN_REPORT_ Labor_2030.pdf > 23.04.2018.

235
Ibid.

236
Wenzel, Eike, "Kolumne_16: Produziert Künstliche Intelligenz noch mehr Ungleichheit und zerstört dadurch unsere Demokratie?", itz, Institut für Trend- und Zukunftsforschung, 17.02.2018, http://www. zukunftpassiert.de/kolumne_16-produziert-kuenstliche-intelli-genz-noch-mehr-ungleichheit-und-zerstoert-dadurch-unsere-de-mokratie/ > 24.04.2018.

237
Harari, Yuval Noah,< in the myth of freedom>, 2018, https:// www.theguardian.com/books/2018/sep/14/yuval-noah-hara-ri-the-new-threat-to-liberal-democracy, 10.10.2018.

238
https://www.forbes.com/sites/forbescoachescouncil/2017/12/13/ promoting-employee-happiness-benefits-everyone/#413094d2581a > 02.10.2018

Notes

<u>Notes</u>

Lightning Source UK Ltd.
Milton Keynes UK
UKHW030636170720
366698UK00010B/1507

9 783981 924947